"Jena Forehand is calling our generation to step up. If we have experienced a deep walk with the Spirit long enough to have time's perspective—to have a context bigger than right now, in this compressed frame—then we owe it to the next generation to pass it on. Jena reminds me that my life can infect the life of another with a passionate pursuit of the present-tense Jesus."

—JENNIFER KENNEDY DEAN, executive director,
The Praying Life Foundation; author of *Live a Praying Life*

jena forehand

living deeper

WOMEN HELPING WOMEN WALK WITH GOD

NAVPRESS

Discipleship Inside Out®

© 2013 by Jena Forehand

All rights reserved. No part of this publication may be reproduced in any form without written permission from NavPress, P.O. Box 35001, Colorado Springs, CO 80935. www.navpress.com

NAVPRESS and the NAVPRESS logo are registered trademarks of NavPress. Absence of ® in connection with marks of NavPress or other parties does not indicate an absence of registration of those marks.

ISBN-13: 978-1-61291-428-2

Cover design by Lux Creative

Some of the anecdotal illustrations in this book are true to life and are included with the permission of the persons involved. All other illustrations are composites of real situations, and any resemblance to people living or dead is coincidental.

Unless otherwise identified, all Scripture quotations in this publication are taken from *THE MESSAGE* (msg). Copyright © 1993, 1994, 1995, 1996, 2000, 2001, 2002. Used by permission of NavPress Publishing Group. Other versions used include: the *Holy Bible, New International Version*® (niv®), Copyright © 1973, 1978, 1984, 2011 by Biblica, used by permission of Zondervan, all rights reserved worldwide; the *Holy Bible*, New Living Translation (nlt), copyright © 1996, 2004, 2007. Used by permission of Tyndale House Publishers, Inc., Wheaton, Illinois 60189. All rights reserved; and the King James Version (kjv).

Forehand, Jena.
  Living deeper : women helping women walk with God / Jena Forehand.
    pages cm
  Includes bibliographical references.
  ISBN 978-1-61291-428-2
  1. Discipling (Christianity) 2. Mentoring—Religious aspects—Christianity.
3. Christian women—Religious life. I. Title.
  BV4520.F67 2013
  248.8'43—dc23

2013002546

Printed in the United States of America

1 2 3 4 5 6 7 8 / 18 17 16 15 14 13

contents

author's note

You may be wondering, *Why a chapter 0?* Because most people skip the introduction or preface, I didn't want anyone to skip the backstory of how this book came into being. So I wanted to name the introduction something that was intriguing and unique. I was speaking to a young man in the armed forces, and he told me about the phrase "alert and oriented times zero."

When someone gets injured and has lost some of his or her mental faculties, the condition is described as "alert and oriented times" and then a number is placed at the end to indicate how severe the disorientation is. The worst condition is known as "alert and oriented times zero." When he shared that with me, it made me think of how I was "alert and oriented times zero" when it came to the spiritual state of our nation and world. God has made me fully aware of this in recent days, and that is why I couldn't help but write this book.

I pray that God will use my writings to orient you to me personally and to the call God has placed on my life. I hope that you will come to see how negatively today's younger generations view the church and Christianity. I believe that as you read, the Holy Spirit will stir the same desires in you that He has in me. So don't miss chapter 0! Otherwise, you'll miss the foundation for the rest of the book.

0

deep calls to deep

Deep calls to deep in the roar of your waterfalls; all your waves
and breakers have swept over me.

— PSALM 42:7, NIV

It's been said that the more you know the heavenly Father, the less you
feel you know Him and the more you desire of Him. I can certainly
attest that this is true. Over the course of my life, I have experienced
taking the loving hand of the Father as He has led me into deeper
waters with Him. This book is yet another journey with my Father
deeper into His heart. I pray it encourages you to take His hand and
let Him take you deeper too.

How I Got Here

In July 2004, God said to me, "I'm calling out a remnant of people
who will follow Me." I had no idea what this meant, why it was said
to me, or how in the world this would be fulfilled. For the next seven
years, I zealously took matters into my own hands. Though my desires
were sincere, I had grown impatient with God. I developed unrealistic
expectations that were outside of God's timetable and out from under
His protection and anointing. And though some great things
happened that advanced the kingdom, it never felt as if I ever reached
my "sweet spot." And my heart yearned for it—whatever "it" was
supposed to be.

In May 2011, I boarded a flight to Colorado Springs, Colorado, to share the longings of my heart with NavPress, the publishing arm of The Navigators. I knew it would be a long flight from Birmingham, Alabama, so I ran into a Christian bookstore to grab something to read. I was drawn to a book that describes the generations that are coming behind me. I settled into my seat, turned on my overhead light, and opened to page one. By the time I arrived in Colorado, the book was read, the waters of truth had saturated my heart, and the calling out into deeper waters had begun inside of me. There was no turning back. No throwing in the towel. I knew what "it" was—finally—and there was no question of its validity. This was a personal invitation from the Lord, and I was jumping in with both feet.

As I awakened the morning of the meeting, I grabbed my Bible to read my Scriptures for the day, and God graciously blessed me with the words from Proverbs 13:12: "Hope deferred makes the heart sick, but a longing fulfilled is a tree of life" (NIV). I realized at that moment that the words the Lord had spoken to me seven years before were now being brought to completion. He had been preparing me all this time for this moment, and I had a fire in my belly that was inextinguishable. I had to find a way to motivate women of older generations to help the new generation, called the Millennials, learn how to walk with God.

Who Are the Millennials?

There is a generation coming behind us that has been labeled the "Millennials." They are the largest generation yet, comprised of anyone born approximately between 1980 and 2000. By the 2008 election of

President Barack Obama, they proved that when they unite, they can make a powerful change. They are fascinating people: smart, focused, and determined to make a lasting impact on the earth. Their aim is not to make a lot of money as much as it is to do something good in the world. They would rather take a lower paying job and feel as though what they are doing is impactful than take a higher paying job that is not. Family and other relationships are a priority to them. I *love* this generation.

> ## Thoughts from Present-Day Leaders
> They combine the teamwork ethic of the Boomers with the can-do attitude of the Veterans and the technological savvy of the Xers. At first glance, and even at second glance, the Millennial Generation may be ideal citizens.
> — RON ZEMKE, CLAIRE RAINES, AND BOB FILIPCZAK, IN *GENERATIONS AT WORK*

But here's the problem: Only about 13 percent of them say that the church and Christianity is important to them.[1] Now think about it: If they are the largest generation, and they have already proved that their unified efforts can produce huge effects toward change, then what could happen if the other 87 percent developed a relationship with Jesus Christ? What if the Millennials came together, not to elect a president, but to receive and then give away the love of Jesus? The results would turn this world upside down!

The Lord had me — hook, line, and sinker.

Understanding the "Why"

I began to question why these Millennials do not see faith in Christ as essential, and why they do not come to church to be encouraged by a group of people who are on the same journey. Why are they missing from our church pews, and how did we miss seeing them slip out the back door? God led me to the book of Judges. Here, He showed me that there once was a generation who had seen all of the works of God: the freeing of the Israelites from the oppression of the Egyptians, as well as the parting of the Red Sea. But that generation was now dead and gone. This is what the Scripture says next: "Eventually that entire generation died and was buried. Then another generation grew up that didn't know anything of GOD or the work he had done for Israel" (Judges 2:10). There had once been a generation who had experienced a firsthand faith, but they had given birth to a generation with no faith at all.

I became sick to my stomach. I knew the truth: My generation had become deadly silent as a new generation emerged who currently neither knows God nor desires the things of God. It is true—and it is on me. *Another problem revealed itself:* If the older generations do not start going deeper with God and taking the younger generations with them, they are going to leave the next generation with no faith at all, and the church as we know it will cease to exist.

As my heart filled with great conviction, I asked myself a much-needed question: *How and why in the world did we get here?* There was a time when we, the church, were a vibrant, living organism, prominent in our culture and making a major impact on individuals, communities, nations, and the world. What in the world happened?

I recalled Isaiah 43:18-19, which says, "Forget about what's happened; don't keep going over old history. Be alert, be present. I'm about to do something brand-new." This was definitely a brand-new thing springing up inside of me!

So often we find ourselves riddled with the "should have, could have, and would haves" of our past, and yet God tells us to forget it, to stop getting bogged down in it, and to move forward with what He has for us. It is only valuable to take a look at our past if we can learn from it for the "new thing" ahead of us. I had a choice to make. I could wallow in the wonderings of the past, or I could take an educational look back in order to move forward productively. I chose the latter. Here are my findings and what I gleaned for our future.

What Happened in the Church?

Insights from the Millennials

I was trained with rules: Don't have sex; don't get drunk; don't do this or that; don't, don't, don't . . . but no one ever told me why. They never showed me what the Bible said about why.

— MOLLY, FROM ALABAMA

For me, as far back as the late sixties, life as I knew it in the South was laid-back. Socially, doors were left open, even unlocked at night, and the front porch swing or rocker was an invitation for conversation at any point during the day. Many a problem was solved over a glass of syrupy sweet tea or freshly squeezed lemonade, and many a tear was dried with a gentle hand and a heartfelt prayer. The local church building was the family's "home away from home"—if they were not actually at home, they were at the church. I received my first "whippin'" at the church for tickling people's legs under the pews during Wednesday night prayer meeting. You lived, worked, shopped, and went to school and church with the same group of people. Thus, when you got a "whippin'," it could have come from any of these folks, because they all knew you, your family, and how they expected you to behave. There was no hiding. The Bible taught how you were supposed to live, and you were expected as a Christian to live that way. Though there seemed to be very little grace coming from the church, the Bible was preached every single Sunday, with Sunday school, training union, and the like all centered on the Bible.

Insights from the Millennials

Lots of tradition, little explanation, lots of control, little freedom: Church to me was a bunch of rules and very cold.

— DIANNA, FROM SOUTH CAROLINA

There was always something going on at the church: Sunday morning services, Sunday school, and worship with dinner on the grounds afterward—along with whenever a good reason presented itself; Sunday night training and worship; Monday night committee meetings; Tuesday night visitation; Wednesday night supper, prayer meeting, and choir practice; Thursday night family night; and Friday night making a meal for someone around town or preparing your home for Saturday's baby shower, wedding reception, or community outreach project. Life revolved around the local church building, the people in it, and those around it who needed help. And in this environment, three innate needs were met for every person: connection, counsel, and content, all based on the authority of the Bible.

Insights from the Millennials

I don't think I ever went to church with my parents. I think my grandparents on my mom's side attended church occasionally, but I'm not really sure about that. Look, I know you are trying to understand the religious preferences of my generation, so I'm trying to shoot straight with you. But the bottom line is that I really don't think of religion or church that much. It's just not on my radar.

— ARDEN, FROM ALABAMA

Over the course of time, however, for innumerable reasons, people began to go inside their homes and lock the doors. People began to shift their focus onto themselves instead of others. The family unit became inundated with a media craze that went from broadcasting wholesome, virtuous messages to rebellious, out-of-control propaganda, initiating divisiveness. Families began to move from their close-knit communities to venture out, looking for better jobs, more money, and greater opportunities for their children. A new personal pursuit had emerged and taken precedence over the mission of the church: to make a better life for your family by chasing power, prestige, and wealth. The church and its activities, along with its "80/20" mentality (80 percent of church members do nothing, while 20 percent do the work) caused major burnout for those who were working in the church. Activities in the local church began to dwindle. Churches began to provide only Sunday morning worship services to free up its membership for more "family time." But that mentality backfired, because people just filled their newly acquired free time with other activities, like worldly entertainment and children's activities that appealed to a "bigger and better" and "popularity contest" mind-set. And life as we knew it began to unravel.

Insights from the Millennials

I have an iPhone and I would die without it. It's the most important thing in my life.

— LIZZIE, FROM FLORIDA

I just got my iPhone for Christmas, actually, from my boyfriend. And it's probably my favorite thing ever. It's the best possession I've ever owned. It blows my mind every day at everything it can do.

— LINDSEY, FROM NEW YORK

Although I would prefer not to make sweeping generalizations, it is true that today, for the most part, we live in a very closed, protective, and self-centered society. There is little or no interaction with other people except for surface and superficial dialogue — usually intended for personal gain. People are more lonely, depressed, and even suicidal than ever before. They lack deep, loving, and caring relationships. A sense of community is at an all-time low. Counseling services are flooded with clients because people now have to pay someone to listen to them and help them sort things out (even though professional counselors rarely serve syrupy sweet tea or freshly squeezed lemonade!).

The local church, in many cases, has become a weak, ear-tickling, and carnal social club concerned only with how its baptism numbers look in comparison to those of other churches in the area. Too many pastors are pressured to not run off the "rich people" by saying anything too harsh, and they seek to please everyone who threatens to leave when things are not done their way. Church splits have also increased dramatically, further implicating the church as a divided group who can't get past its pettiness to take care of others who need Jesus. Church denominations further separate the church and actually compete with each other, though they say they are all on the same team. Churches within the same denomination compare and compete even more, not letting their church members be a part of another church's events for fear they might like their facility better and move their membership. Women's Bible studies frequently leave their attendees frustrated because they expect connection, counsel, and deep biblical content to all take place in a one-hour time slot. But there is either too much Bible study and not enough talking time, or there is too much talking time and not enough Bible study. And the older generation of churchgoers are either upset with the new way of "doing church" and are leaving, or they are adapting yet feeling tossed to the side as the new, more talented, tech-savvy, and educated generation takes over. Would you agree?

Wisdom from Past Generations
Only a disciple can make a disciple.
— A. W. TOZER, TWENTIETH-CENTURY PASTOR, PREACHER, AND AUTHOR

As a part of one of the older generations, maybe you currently have more on your plate than you can manage. Or maybe you have nothing on your plate and are looking for something to make life worthwhile. Believe it or not, whether you are at either extreme, both can leave you dry, empty, and thirsty. You know that there's got to be more to life. You are not alone. Psalm 42 tells us, "As the deer pants for streams of water, so my soul pants for you, my God. My soul thirsts for God, for the living God. . . . Deep calls to deep in the roar of your waterfalls" (NIV, verses 1-2,7). God sees the deep places within you and wants to take you into the deeper waters with Him. The depths of who He is are calling out to the deep places within you. He wants to saturate you with His love and then pour you out onto others around you, naturally, intentionally — and eternally. The question is, will you let Him?

Our Effect on Millennials

Wisdom from Past Generations

The gospel must be preached afresh and told in new ways to every generation, since every generation has its own unique questions. The gospel must constantly be forwarded to a new address, because the recipient is repeatedly changing his place of residence.

— HELMUT THIELICKE, TWENTIETH-CENTURY GERMAN PROTESTANT THEOLOGIAN

The choices we've made in the past have definitely affected the next generation. Millennials have been changed as they watched the lives of their parents and grandparents unfold. These young people have witnessed divorce, manipulation, "easy outs" at the cost of unborn children's lives, blurring lines in gender and sexual orientation, as well as hypocrisy among so-called Christians. Even many church leaders have had the facade of their Christianity exposed for the world to see. Many of these young people have become untrusting, cynical, and judgmental. They are choosing to live together instead of marry because it's "safe" and they can get out of the relationship more easily. Their reasoning and justification may spring from churchgoing parents who divorced and caused themselves and their children incredible pain. There is no commitment and therefore no need to trust or risk in a relationship. If it doesn't work out, no harm done. Intimate relationships are not a given, only sex. These young people may be "spiritual," but they are not "religious." They are averse to the church and are sickened by the hypocrisy of the local church, which proclaims the love of Jesus but does not practice it. They view the church as a negative, divisive, and argumentative group of people, and they want no part of it. Sounds harsh, doesn't it? But isn't it true? Are we to blame?

Church, we have a problem.

Our great God says that He works all things together for the good (see Romans 8:28). So, even in their adverse attitude toward the church, I have also seen in them a God-given desire for deep intimacy in their relationships. They long to learn from older generations. Their self-confidence, which sometimes borders on arrogance, can be channeled into high levels of productivity. They are ambitious and visionary. They are also willing to roll up their sleeves and work hard to see their visions accomplished. They want a religion that is *real*. They long to break the trend of broken families, but they don't know how to do it. They are willing to listen, but they also want to be accepted, loved, and heard. And those who do consider Christianity important desire a radical change in the church and want to practice the Christianity of the Bible, moving back to its roots and origins. They have a fierce devotion to Bible study, a sense of fervency for a relevant prayer life, and a deep commitment to minister to others locally, nationally, and internationally—and they are willing to forfeit any personal or material gain to see this happen. These Millennials need a real, intimate, and genuine relationship with the Father, just as we do. Some things may be different between the generations, but in many ways, we speak the same language.

So here is what we are left with, the problems for which we need to find a solution:

- The church is currently dying a slow death because the next generation, the Millennials, want no part of it; when the older generation dies off, so will the church.
- Older generation church members are suffering from either burnout or from feelings of disillusionment and purposelessness.
- The church is riddled with division both within and between denominations, thus appearing separatist and elitist to outsiders.

Based on this, things might look pretty dismal for the church and its future.

God's Heart in All of This

God loves the church. He loves it so much that He sent Jesus to die for it. Why, even Jesus' last prayer was for us, His bride, the church.

In John 17, Jesus said to the Father,

> I'm praying not only for them
> But also for those who will believe in me
> Because of them and their witness about me.
> The goal is for all of them to become one heart and mind—
> Just as you, Father, are in me and I in you,
> So they might be one heart and mind with us.
> Then the world might believe that you, in fact, sent me.
> The same glory you gave me, I gave them,
> So they'll be as unified and together as we are—
> I in them and you in me.
> Then they'll be mature in this oneness,
> And give the godless world evidence
> That you've sent me and loved them
> In the same way you've loved me. (verses 20-23)

I've always believed that the first words of a person's life and the last words of a person's life are central. I remember as a child the words my parents said to me, "Be kind to all; forgive; your word is your honor; treat others better than yourself." Their words were foundational to who I would become. I also remember the last words of my grandmother as she died. Her words carried a great sense of urgency: "Jena, never lose sight of the importance of family. Love your husband. Love your babies, and take care of your mama; she's *my* baby."

At 8:58 a.m. on September 11, 2001, Brian Sweeney, a businessman who had once flown F-14s for the navy, was on an airphone trying to reach his wife, Julie. She wasn't home, so he said good-bye into the answering machine. Moments later, Sweeney's plane, United Flight 175 from Boston to Los Angeles, crashed into New York's World Trade Center. What did he say when he knew he had only moments left to live? "Hey, Jules, this is Brian. I'm on an airplane that's been hijacked. If things don't go well, and it's not looking good, I just want you to know I absolutely love you. I want you to do good, go have good times. The same to my parents and everybody. And I just totally love you and I'll see you when you get here. Bye, babe. I hope I call you."

Jesus knew that He was about to die too. Here He is in His very last moments, with an opportunity to say what was most important and urgent to those He was leaving behind. And in Jesus' last hours on earth, what was His message to us? He prayed that the church would be *one*. Why? So the world would believe and know the love of God through His people living in a loving, unified relationship with one another. Jesus prayed that we, as the body of Christ, would be unified to take His love all over the world.

Jesus has answered many of our prayers. What an awesome thought that we could be a part of answering His! It is one thing to know that we can have faith in Him, but it is quite another to think that He has faith in us to reach others with His love. Do we fight for unity in our individual churches, denominations, communities, states, and nation? Are we coming together to make His name great so others can believe? Have we done our part in answering His prayer?

But what if this deep longing of Jesus could be answered by *you*? What if there was a way for you to take the lead in inciting, exciting, and unifying the older generations to reach out to the younger generation? What if the Millennial generation then joined the church and together we made a tremendous impact upon this earth? And what if the means to do it were not found in the "tips and techniques" that have long been the mantra in our local churches, but rather found in the example of Jesus Himself? And furthermore, what if, in doing this, you found the fulfillment you've been longing for to quench your thirsty and empty soul? How different would your life be?

Thoughts from Present-Day Leaders

Whether you be a parent, aunt, uncle, godparent, grandparent, or spiritual parent, you have a tremendous privilege and command in God's Word to make a difference by passing the baton of faith to the next generation, imprinting God's love on the next generation.

— ESTHER BURROUGHS, AUTHOR OF *ENGRAVED BY GRACE*

I believe new life would come to the church. I believe that the older generations would find new purpose, excitement, and personal fulfillment, as Jesus intended. I believe that there would be a revival of the church to unify for one common purpose: the glory of our great God. And I believe that God would help us reach the next generations, who will then passionately partner with us to turn this world upside down for the cause of Christ. The Bible tells us, "Stand at the crossroads and look; ask for the ancient paths, ask where the good way is, and walk in it, and you will find rest for your souls" (Jeremiah 6:16, NIV). Sisters in Christ Jesus our Lord, we stand at a crossroads. The future of the next generations — our children, our grandchildren, our great-grandchildren—is in our hands. The damage has been done as we have walked our own paths, but I believe God is calling out a remnant of people who will follow Him authentically and teach the next generations to do the same.

Will you choose to walk the "good path" so that the generations that come behind can follow you and find real rest for their souls in a time when there is none? The invitation is yours. How will you answer?

I am confident that if the older generations lead the next generation to a deepening walk with Jesus, it will not only give the older generations a united purpose and deep fulfillment, but it will also turn the hearts of the Millennials toward Jesus. It will unite them with the older generations, reviving and returning the church to the vibrant, living organism that will make a powerful impact on this earth to advance the love of Christ throughout the world.

God is calling out a remnant of people who will *follow Him!* He is calling out a group of people who will reach the future generations, so that the church can be revived, so that the church will thrive again, and so that many will believe and know that there is a God who desperately loves them. I believe the time is now. I believe that God is stirring the church, the older generations, to begin living in deeper waters with Him and taking the next generations with us!

In typing these words, I am remembering the days when I wanted so desperately to learn to swim. I would stand at the edge of the pool for what seemed like forever, as my emotions roiled in an odd mix of fear and elation all at once. I saw others swimming and having a great time, and I wanted to do that too. But I was also scared of the unknown and it held me back for the longest time. It wasn't until my mother or father got into the pool, held out his or her arms, and began calling out to me, that I felt safe enough to take the plunge.

Do you feel like that too? Maybe you've been standing on the edge of the pool, wanting to live in deeper relationship with Jesus, as you've seen others walk in abundance with Him, but fear has had you stuck on the side of the pool. Or maybe you've wanted to do something to bring the love of God to others and have been standing on the very edge of the pool, waiting for your chance to just jump right in! Be of good courage — your Father is standing in the deep, holding out His arms, and calling out to you. He will lead you, guide you, and show you how to go into the deep and take others with you.

Insights from the Millennials

I have come to church a thousand times, continually thinking that one of these days I will find the "more" of the Christian life, and yet I seem to always leave lacking.

— Missy, from Florida

In John 5, the story is told of a man who had been lying by the pool of Bethesda (meaning "House of Kindness") for thirty-eight years. That pool offered healing to the first person who could get in, once an angel of the Lord stirred the waters. The problem was, he couldn't get in by himself. He needed help. Can you imagine waiting thirty-eight years for your turn to find wholeness and healing? Yet he had been lured into hoping and believing that at that pool he would find what he had longed for, for so long. Although he found hopelessness instead of hope after all those years of waiting, he stayed poolside, because there still was a slight chance of change, and besides, it was comfortable — it was all he knew.

Can you relate? Have you ever felt the inward struggle of coming to church and being so disappointed because you had heard what God could do to give you abundant life, but quite honestly, you never found it? But because it is comfortable and familiar, you walk in and out and the condition of your heart never changes? Can you imagine others who have lain by the pool of the church (the supposed "House of Kindness"), waiting for years for someone to help them get in and find the deeper things of God?

Then Jesus enters the scene and asks the man, "Do you want to be well?" This man, sick for thirty-eight years, answered, "I can't, because . . ." Sometimes I believe that we settle for a life that is far less than God intended because He asks us a question and we answer, "I can't, because . . ." Today, I believe God is asking you, "Will you take My hand and let Me lead you into living deeper with Me? Will you take up where I left off and go to those who are lying by the pool and need to find healing?" How many people do you know right now who are lying beside the pool and are looking for the kindness of God to come and help them get in? Will you now, when you are needed the most, stop at your own fearful insecurities and inadequacies? Or will you act upon that for which you have so deeply been called and to which you so strongly believe?

Thoughts from Present-Day Leaders

Jesus said that He completed His work by making disciples. Your work is complete when the person you are discipling can make a disciple.

— JIM PUTMAN, SENIOR PASTOR, REAL LIFE MINISTRIES

Jesus said, "I glorified you [the Father] on earth by completing down to the last detail what you assigned me to do" (John 17:4). What is that work? To make disciples. Jesus then prayed for us to come together in making disciples, strengthening the church, while declaring God's deep love to the world. He completed the work He was sent to accomplish. Will you accomplish yours? The deep heart of the Father is calling out to the depths of your heart. Deep calls to deep. Are you ready and willing to get off the side of the pool and jump in, to do your part in changing our culture? Are you willing to begin living in deeper relationship with God and helping others do the same? If so, then let's talk about the *how*. How will we reach the next generation, give the older generations a newfound passion and purpose, and bring the church together in unity to do big things for the glory of God? First, let's take a look at the generations and their differences, and see how the church has missed it thus far. Then we'll take a closer look at the task before us. Does this task sound too big? Don't worry. It is Jesus' prayer, and He will both equip and empower us to make this a reality, through one simple word: discipleship.

Deeper Reflections

At the end of each chapter, I offer discussion questions for you to consider. It is my prayer that you will not only be reading this book for the ones you will disciple. I pray that you will also be surprised that as you learn how to disciple, and even begin discipling, you too will be being discipled.

1. What do you think about the younger generation and its positive and negative impacts upon our culture? Have you given up hope for them to want a vibrant relationship with Jesus? Or do you see positive signs that they can be reached with the love of Christ?
2. How many non-Christians, especially those between the ages of eighteen and thirty-five, are you friends with and praying for?
3. What do you see as the primary differences between the "older" generations and the "younger" ones that are following? What might be the positive and negative results of these differences? How might these differences be bridged, for the sake of the church and the gospel?
4. What fears and insecurities do you face when thinking about discipling the next generation? To what do you say, "I can't, because . . ."? How might God respond to this statement? What

else might be holding you back? How can you trust God to help you overcome these obstacles?

5. What is your attitude toward those who are outside the faith in our emerging culture? Hope and optimism? Or callousness and dismissiveness? Ask God to give you a heart of discipleship for the lost members of the Millennial generation.

1

agree to "follow me"

Real religion, the kind that passes muster before God the Father, is this: Reach out to the homeless and loveless in their plight, and guard against corruption from the godless world.

— JAMES 1:27

Genesis 11 tells us the story of the Tower of Babel. People had migrated to the region of Shinar (Babylonia). There, they came together and built a tower that they believed would make their name great—would make them famous. The problem was that the people had come together in unity, but for all the wrong reasons. In response, God scattered the people, causing them to speak different languages, making them unable to complete the task they had undertaken. Here's the point: When we seek to make our own name great, God scatters. But when we seek to make His name great, He unites.

Wisdom from Past Generations

Be united with other Christians. A wall with loose bricks is not good. The bricks must be cemented together.

— CORRIE TEN BOOM, AUTHOR AND NAZI HOLOCAUST SURVIVOR

The truth is, there are a lot of things on which churches disagree and divide. Many a church has been brought down when its agenda became all about making its own name great. But the one thing I think the entire church would agree on is that Christians are commissioned to make disciples. In fact, it must be the one thing on which we all agree and unite, in order to make the name of Jesus great. Matthew 28:18-22 tells us,

> Jesus, undeterred, went right ahead and gave his charge: "God authorized and commanded me to commission you: Go out and train everyone you meet, far and near, in this way of life, marking them by baptism in the threefold name: Father, Son, and Holy Spirit. Then instruct them in the practice of all I have commanded you. I'll be with you as you do this, day after day after day, right up to the end of the age."

Jesus Is Calling Us Out!

Jesus sent forth His disciples to go and make more disciples. His desire was a group of unified disciples, making more unified disciples, so the church would be a strong, unified body of believers. The sole goal of the church was to love God and love others, turning this world upside down, as more and more disciples were made. Jesus was inaugurating a revolution! That's why He said in John 14:12, "The person who trusts me will not only do what I'm doing but even greater [as in quantity] things, because I, on my way to the Father, am giving you the same work to do that I've been doing." He also said, "It's better for you that I leave. If I don't leave, the Friend won't come. But if I go, I'll send him to you" (John 16:7). Jesus was saying that once He left, the Holy Spirit would empower every believer to go make disciples, empowering more disciples to go and make more disciples!

Wisdom from Past Generations

The first order ever given to man was that he "be fruitful and multiply." In other words, he was to reproduce after his own kind. God said, "Multiply. I want more just like you, more in My own image."

— DAWSON TROTMAN, EVANGELIST AND FOUNDER OF THE NAVIGATORS

Throughout the Bible, God has used the physical to explain the spiritual. Even Jesus used parabolic teaching to help His disciples understand what the kingdom of God was like. I would like to submit that since creation, God has made discipleship a central focus, when He blessed Adam and Eve and told them to "Prosper! Reproduce! Fill Earth! Take charge!" (Genesis 1:28). Even then, I believe that God was speaking to spiritual fruitfulness and multiplication just as much, if not more, than physical. God really came up with the multiplication process long before marketing pyramids did!

Discipleship. The word is mentioned and we begin a dialogue in our heads: "What does that even mean?" "Am I a disciple?" "Have I ever even been discipled myself?" and "How do you even do it?" Right? Yeah, me too.

So, what is a disciple? We throw that term around a lot, but we may never really know what it means, implies, or requires. The word *disciple* translates the Greek word *mathetes* and simply means "learner," or "student."

Wisdom from Past Generations

Let this be thy whole endeavor, this thy only prayer, this thy desire — that thou mayest be stripped of all selfishness, and with entire simplicity follow Jesus only.
— THOMAS A KEMPIS, FIFTEENTH-CENTURY AUTHOR AND BISHOP OF THE CHURCH

In the days of Jesus, the word *disciple* offered an incredible sense of belonging, honor, and approval. Jewish history tells us that boys who were born into fairly affluent homes would receive the special privilege of going to the temple courts and sitting before the teachers of the law, learning from them as they taught orally at the temple. Many began this process before they reached five years of age, and by the age of thirty they had the authority to teach others. (That's why Jesus, following Jewish tradition, began His ministry at the age of thirty.)

Now, at some point during this timeline of events, a scribe or teacher of the law (known as a rabbi) might notice a particular young man whom he believed was exceptional; he even believed the young man could possibly take his place once he died. When he was convinced that he wanted that young man to become his apprentice, he would say two little words: "Follow me." Immediately the young man would leave his father and mother and follow his rabbi, taking on his interpretation of the law, known as his "yoke." The new disciple would follow so closely behind his rabbi that others would offer this blessing: "May the dust of your rabbi fall upon you!"

Have you ever looked at Matthew 4:19-20 through these lenses? Jesus was walking along the shore [the edge of the pool], saw Peter and Andrew, and called to them, saying, "Follow Me, and I will make you fishers of men." At once, they left their nets and followed Him.

Have you ever wondered why Simon Peter and Andrew would just drop what they were doing immediately to follow a man they had never even met before? It was because they longed for value and a sense of belonging. They would have loved to sit on the temple steps and learn. But they were born into families that required them to go out and work. They watched the other young men leave home to learn at the temple, while they spent their time out on the fishing boats. This had to give them a sense of rejection, even purposelessness. Then a man named Jesus came to them and spoke with words of authority, the same words the scribes and teachers of the law would say: "Follow Me." And immediately they left their nets and followed their new Rabbi, Jesus.

They also left their fathers and mothers. Jesus said, "Anyone who comes to me but refuses to let go of father, mother, spouse, children, brothers, sisters—yes, even one's own self!—can't be my disciple" (Luke 14:26).

They took on His interpretation of the Word and walked in obedience to it. After all, Jesus *was* the Word, so He was perfectly accurate! He knew that living deeper in relationship with Him as His disciple was the only way to truly live.

Are you tired? Worn out? Burned out on religion? Come to me. Get away with me and you'll recover your life. I'll show you how to take a real rest. Walk with me and work with me — watch how I do it. Learn the unforced rhythms of grace. I won't lay anything heavy or ill-fitting on you. Keep company with me and you'll learn to live freely and lightly. (Matthew 11:28-30)

As disciples of Jesus, they walked so closely to Him that they watched His every move and did exactly what He did, so that the very dust of their Rabbi fell upon them. Jesus did the very same thing, showing them an example. Jesus said, "I'm telling you this straight. The Son can't independently do a thing, only what he sees the Father doing. What the Father does, the Son does. The Father loves the Son and includes him in everything he is doing" (John 5:19-20).

This is why the disciples jumped at the opportunity! Maybe, for the very first time, someone had seen worth in them. Someone thought that they could make a difference. Someone had restored in them some dignity. Someone was calling them to a place of belonging, acceptance, and value. They were no longer invisible or unimportant. They were charged with a great purpose — to make disciples of the Lord Jesus Christ.

And this is what Jesus was saying to you when He called you to follow Him too!

In the movie *The Help*, a maid named Abilene speaks words of value into the daughter of the family for which she works: "You is kind, you is smart, you is important." Sometimes it's just good to be reminded of that!

Older generations, Jesus sees in you great worth. He sees great potential inside of you that He put there when He created you. He sees an honor and a dignity in you that only come from what He placed inside of you. And He offers you a place of belonging if you will continue what He began on this earth: the making of disciples. Until you take your last breath, God still has things He wants to accomplish through you, in the life of another. The time is now. Satan is urgently out to destroy us because he knows his time is short (see Revelation 12:12). The last days are upon us whether we want to face them or not. O God, that You would give Your people a strong sense of urgency to disciple the next generations before it is too late!

How Do We Do It?

So you've come to the pool and you are allowing the Lord to take you by the hand and lead you to living in deeper waters of relationship with Him. Now the question becomes, who are you going to get to go with you . . . and how? Our job, then, is to understand the people of this generation, the process of discipling them, and how to invite them into the pool of becoming a disciple of Jesus along with us.

Wisdom from Past Generations

Those who teach by their doctrine must teach by their life, or else they pull down with one hand what they build up with another.
— MATTHEW HENRY, SEVENTEENTH-CENTURY BIBLICAL COMMENTATOR

Understanding the Next Generation

I have said many times that if we misdefine something, we will mishandle it. My husband, Dale, is a practical joker. As a child, he knew his father was deathly afraid of snakes. One night, he went outside and wrapped a rubber snake around the side mirror of his father's truck. At dusk, when his dad walked out to his truck, he was terrified to see the snake, which appeared to be real. He took out his nine-iron golf club and hit that rubber snake so hard that he tore the mirror off the side of the truck!

The following Easter, Dale's father walked into their den and there, sitting on top of the VCR, was that same rubber snake — or so he thought! He reached to grab that old rubber snake and it turned out to be a real snake that hissed and jumped at him! He did about three backflips and ran for his gun! You see, when he defined the rubber snake as real, he mishandled it and ripped off his mirror. When he defined the real snake as fake, he about got himself bit!

So it is when it comes to people. If we misdefine them, or misunderstand them, we will mishandle them and respond in ways that are not beneficial or productive.

A Quick Look

What are the priorities of the Millennial generation? The answer to that question is easy: relationships. Relationships are important because of their connection to their families. Millennials also see the world as a much smaller place because they can visit anywhere in the world (either in person or via the Internet). And they are connected to people through the new media in ways that no other generation has been able to do.

Education is a high priority for Millennials. They do not want education so that they can make more money, but rather they are in a quest to find real answers that they cannot seem to find anywhere else. Millennials want to make money, but they are not driven by money. Their motivation for education and career is driven more by family and friends. One word that often surfaces is the word *flexibility*. They see money as a means to do what they want to do. At the same time, they reject the "keeping up with the Joneses" mentality that often drives their parents.

Thoughts from Present-Day Leaders

The Millennial Generation will entirely recast the image of youth from downbeat and alienated to upbeat and engaged — with potentially seismic consequences for America.

— NEIL HOWE AND WILLIAM STRAUSS, AUTHORS OF *MILLENNIALS RISING*

The political orientation of Millennials will no doubt influence elections. A greater percentage of this generation will become eligible to vote in each new election cycle. Politics is often a priority to them because they see the urgent need for change and want to work hard at making a difference for the future.

Last, and yet one of the most important points, is that Millennials are faced with much brokenness, and they are focused on finding healing. With television and music reverberating much drama, they try to create their own drama if they are currently not experiencing any. Because drama appears to be the norm, when they don't feel elation, love, joy, or excitement, they create it for themselves. Sex, cutting, relationship games, lying, backstabbing, gossip, and the like are at an all-time high among Millennials. Consequently, their distrust and anxiety levels are higher than those of any previous generation. They are desperately searching for healing from their emotional, relational, and sexual wounds.

If you want to connect with Millennials, spend some time with them. Build a relationship that includes both talking and listening. Hear their struggles and help them sort through their confusion. Listen to their questions and offer them concrete truth and practical application that truly solves their problems, alleviates their pain, and frees them to life abundant as they learn to walk with God.

A Different and Dynamic Generation
What Is Important to Them:

- Relationships, including parents and their own family members (spouse and children)
- Flexible schedules, so that relationships can be a priority
- Projects and causes to make a lasting impact around them
- Openness and honesty (they hate "fakeness" and can smell it a mile away)
- Productivity, without having to start at the bottom and work their way up
- Finding healing for their brokenness

Meet an amazing Millennial named Victoria. She is beautiful, kindhearted, and compassionate. Her thoughts are never on herself, but rather on those she has a relationship with. They are primary to her and their needs take precedence over her own. I love Victoria. Relationships are the consummation of her existence, and she values them so much that she works hard at making them the best they can be.

How to Communicate with Them:

- Be short, concise, and to the point (they want to hear from you)
- Use bullet points so they can scan and choose what is important enough to read
- Use all social networking available
- Value discussion, not shoving down the throat, demands, or force
- Be genuine, sincere, unpretentious, real
- Listen to them intently and seek to identify and understand

Meet my Millennial friend Kelsey. She is intellectual, witty, and every bit beautiful inside and out! She amazes me by the way she intently listens to what you have to say. I can almost see the wheels in her mind turning as I talk with her. She isn't much of a talker, but boy, when she has something to say, you'd best have a pen around to capture the wisdom. She's not up for small talk. She likes you to cut to the chase and jump into discussion that is real and authentic. This girl is amazing!

How to Lead Them:

- Personally, based on their personality, customized just for them
- Living life before them, setting for them an example to follow, as a mentor

- Living life with them, being accessible to them throughout the day
- With great integrity, being who you say you are, backing up your words with your actions
- Offering fresh and unique ways to experience God
- Entrust them with big responsibilities to prove you believe in them
- Walking along beside them as fellow sojourners, not better than them

Meet Elise: strong, assertive, gorgeous, and confident. She has no problem seeing right through you and calling it out! When she disagrees or wants to challenge what you are saying, she jumps in with both feet. She and I text a lot during the week, and she sees things from a perspective that I never see. She is a delight! We just finished wallpapering a room in my house and enjoyed accomplishing something while spending time together.

Their View of the Pew

It may be hard for the older generations to believe, but we are living in a post-Christian world. To the young people of today, Christianity isn't normal. This is really important to realize, and if you aren't sensing this in our emerging culture, you might be too enclosed in your Christian network and subculture to fully see what's happening.

Thoughts from Present-Day Leaders

Arguably, this is the most consequential generation of young adults, perhaps since the baby boomers, who famously made a lot of noise in the sixties and were part of a countercultural movement.
— PAUL TAYLOR, EXECUTIVE VICE PRESIDENT OF THE PEW RESEARCH CENTER

If you are a boomer or of an older generation and were born into a Christian home, you probably have relationships with people who still share values and beliefs that are more in line with a Christian world, and you might not see the change in emerging generations. If you are younger, were raised in a church, and surround yourself socially only with Christians, then you might not notice this as strongly either. But things have changed slowly, yet dramatically.

That's why it is so important that we think like missionaries. We can no longer assume that everyone who surrounds us knows the name of Jesus or is a Christian.

I had a precious, vivacious young woman enter my home for a new small group who had no idea who Jesus was nor what a "word, a number, and then a colon and then more numbers stood for" (they were actually Scripture references).

Instead of viewing our towns and cities as Christian and feeling that everyone automatically adheres to what we believe, we need to act as missionaries when they enter a different culture. When missionaries enter another culture, they listen, learn, study the spiritual beliefs of the culture, and get a sense of what the culture's values are. They may try to discover what experiences this culture has had with Christians and what the people of the culture think of Christianity. Missionaries in a foreign culture don't practice the faiths or embrace the spiritual beliefs of that culture, but they do respect them, since the missionaries are on the other culture's turf. They ask the Holy Spirit to reveal open opportunities to share their faith in a way that is not obtrusive and offensive, but rather uplifting and encouraging to offer hope where many do not have it. They do not communicate with a preemptory attitude, but they listen and respond in love.

In the same way, we must enter an entirely new culture when we attempt to reach the new generations for Jesus—even the younger people who live in our towns and cities, who attend our churches, or even who live in our own families. Take, for example, the meanings of the following words and how they have changed between adult culture and youth culture today.

Word	Older Generation's Definition	Younger Generation's Definition
Tolerance	Accepting others without agreeing with or sharing their beliefs or lifestyle choices	Accepting that each individual's beliefs, values, lifestyles, and truth claims are equal and not to be questioned
Respect	Giving due consideration to others' beliefs and lifestyle choices without necessarily approving of them	Wholeheartedly applauding others' beliefs or lifestyle choices as their personal freedom to choose
Acceptance	Embracing people just the way they are, but loving them enough not to leave them in a way that is detrimental	Embracing people just the way they are, and leaving them to figure it out on their own
Moral Judgment	Certain things are morally right and wrong as determined by God	We have no right to judge another person's view or behavior
Personal Preference	Preferences of color, food, clothing style, hobbies, etc., are personally determined	Preferences of sexual behaviors, value systems, and beliefs are personally or biologically determined
Personal Rights	Everyone has the right to be treated justly under the law	People have the right to do what they believe is best for themselves
Freedom	Being free to live as you should	Being able to live as you want to
Truth	An absolute standard of right and wrong	A relative standard based on what is right for you

These differences in meaning are symptomatic of a deeper problem — that most of the younger generation do not understand the claims of Jesus or what it means to become a true follower of

Him. What has happened? Why does the "Christianity" that many of our younger people (and some older adults too) adhere to make so little difference in their lives? Is it because they are not attending enough church services and Christian events or that there are not enough seminars and resources available in the form of books, training, or curricula to teach them the truth about Christianity? There is more at their fingertips than ever before, and yet things are getting worse! Although it may sound harsh, George Barna may be right when he says,

> Nothing is more numbing to the Church than the fact that it is mired in a rut of seemingly unfathomable depths. The various creative approaches attempted over the course of this decade have drawn much attention but have produced little, if any, transformational impact . . . although many people attend a church, few Americans are committed to *being* the Church.[1]

I would add that many are attending church and even taking in the knowledge of the Bible, but very few put it into practice, truly becoming disciples who deny themselves, take up their crosses, and follow Him in wholehearted devotion.

What Unchurched Millennials Wish the Church Were Like

1. I wish the church services were not just a sermon or a lecture but a discussion. I don't mind a sermon so long as I have a chance, through a small group or some other form of community, to talk it out and formulate ways in which I can personally apply what was taught into my life. Otherwise, I will feel that I am in a college classroom, getting more information but not necessarily having to assimilate it. *Answer:* Get them into a small group.

Insights from the Millennials

Didn't Jesus spend most of His time in smaller settings with smaller groups? With His twelve disciples? I bet that is where they learned the most from Him, not when He was with the masses or with larger crowds.

— ALICIA, FROM CALIFORNIA

2. I wish the church would respect my intelligence. Older people always talk to me in a way that sounds condescending. They treat me like a mother who is telling me what to do because they are smarter than me. It makes me feel like they think I am stupid. I don't need another mother. I already have one. I need a friend, someone who will walk alongside me, not boss me around. If they would come as open as they expect me to come, they might listen to me and learn from me, too. *Answer:* Give them a voice.

3. I wish the church weren't about the church building. If my body houses Jesus, then I am the temple of God and thus, I am a church. So wherever I am, I must live a life of worship. My life, my talk, and my attitude should not be any different while I am in the church building from how it is when I am out in the world, and yet all those before me seem to act one way at the church building and another in the world. *Answer:* Offer them an example of a lifestyle of integrity.

4. I wish the church services were less programmed and allowed time to think and pray. It just seems that while there must be a schedule or order of worship, no room is left for me to evaluate how this may apply to me and what I will do to make some necessary changes in my life. Sometimes church seems so structured that it makes me wonder if God would be welcomed or would get in the way if He were there. *Answer:* Give them flexibility.

Insights from the Millennials

I don't know why when I go to church they have to constantly say "stand up now" or "sit down now." It feels like I am a kindergartner playing Simon Says, with the pastor telling me what to do in the canned and preplanned program.

— GARY, FROM COLORADO

5. I wish the church were a loving place. Many people are not even smiling at my church. They look mad at the world. They are not nice, welcoming, or cordial, but rather they are stuck up and busy in their own little world, not even acknowledging others. I don't feel accepted but rather rejected. It doesn't make me want to come back at all. *Answer:* Really love them.

6. I wish the church cared for the poor and the environment. It seems as though there is more talk at my church about things being done to help people within the church building instead of beyond the church walls. I very rarely hear anything about helping others who really are in need. There are desperate needs within our communities, and it is time we get out there and help. The poor, the orphans, and the widows are being shifted to rely on the government for help when I thought the Bible said it was a Christian's responsibility to help them. So why aren't we doing anything about it? *Answer:* Join with them in areas of ministry service.

7. I wish the church taught more about Jesus. I want to know who He was; what He did; how He responded to others; what was important to Him; whether He was funny and happy; how He treated the poor, the lonely, and the outcasts; and what moved Him. I want to know how He led His disciples, so I can follow Him better. I need specifics, not broad, conceptual, and topical teachings that sometimes don't apply to me at all. *Answer:* Give them practical theology.

8. I wish the church would hit the hard topics rather than ignoring them both from the pulpit and in the small groups. It seems that leaders either must not have the answers themselves or they are afraid of saying something that might offend someone else. And yet, it would seem that the Bible would sometimes be offensive if we are living contrary to it. I need help with the tough topics, and I need to be able to find my answers in the church, not in the secular media, where it is tainted and twisted. *Answer:* Give them biblical truth.

Insights from the Millennials

I just can't stand leaders who are so full of themselves. I see it in politicians. I see it in the business world. I see it in Hollywood. And I see it in religious leaders. They totally lack integrity. You never know when they are lying.

— LUKE, FROM MISSOURI

9. I wish the church at large would start acting as one body as Christ intended it to be. We are to be one, even though we meet in different buildings. We need to start coming together and be the body of Christ. The division is a huge turnoff to my generation, who longs to work together for change. If we can't do it in the church, we will just find other, secular outlets to do it. At least they are unified. *Answer:* Become unified!

(For a deeper look into the Millennial generation, turn to the appendixes at the back of this book.)

As a member of the older generations, you may not necessarily agree with any of the assessments of the younger generation. They may even offend you. The goal is not for us to agree as much as it is to realize that this is their perspective and understand how their perspective is affecting them. Again, if we don't understand them but rather misdefine them, we will mishandle their hearts and respond to them in ways that do not help and may even harm.

Have you ever heard the phrase "burying your head in the sand"?

It refers to the myth that an ostrich is supposedly so dumb that it believes if it can't see its attacker, then the attacker can't see it. It assumes that if it can't see you, then you can't see it.

Job 39:13-17 says,

The wings of the ostrich flap joyfully,
>   though they cannot compare
>   with the wings and feathers of the stork.
She lays her eggs on the ground
>   and lets them warm in the sand,
unmindful that a foot may crush them,
>   that some wild animal may trample them.
She treats her young harshly, as if they were not hers;
>   she cares not that her labor was in vain,
for God did not endow her with wisdom
>   or give her a share of good sense. (NIV)

We can no longer hide our faces from the facts at hand. We have a generation coming behind us who are being crushed by the wiles of untruth. They do not need us to avoid them because we don't know how to respond to them.

While an ostrich has not been given a brain with good common sense and wisdom, God did give that to us as women, the crown of His creation. There is no greater or more crucial time than now for you to pick up the mantle and reach this next generation with the abundant life that can only be found in walking with God.

They need you; they need *us* to come together in agreement on this one thing: the making of disciples. They want you to take them by the hand and walk with them into the deeper waters of discipleship. They need to see the older generation putting all differences aside for their sake, to make God's name great among them. The next chapters will show you how.

Deeper Reflections

1. Do any of the statistics about the Millennials surprise you? Why or why not?
2. Discuss ways to tap in to the spiritual interest of the Millennials. How can the Christian faith be made more attractive and relevant without compromising the truth?
3. How easy would it be for a twenty-five-year-old to get involved in the life of your church in a significant way? How many hoops would she have to jump through? Can you honestly say you respect someone of that age who is walking with God, and would you help her discover her gifts and empower her to become a leader in your church?
4. How are you building younger leaders in your church? What are you personally doing to help?
5. Is there anything that you or your church is doing that might be getting in the way of God? In what direction do you feel God is moving you to reach the younger generations for Him?
6. Do you see yourself as someone who merely "goes to church" or as a part of a community of local missionaries in today's culture? What could you do to have a more "missional" mind-set toward the younger generations?

2

the process of going deeper

The one indispensable requirement for producing godly, mature Christians is godly, mature Christians.

— KEVIN DEYOUNG

Now that we know more about the Millennials and can better relate to them, we can look at how we disciple them. If we know — truly know — that we are supposed to disciple the next generations, we first need to know what that looks like. How will we help them live deeper with God? And how are we to even go about discipling another person?

One Scripture passage the Lord showed me back in 2004 was Ezekiel 47:1-12. I believe it clearly shows us the *process* of discipleship:

The man brought me back to the entrance of the temple, and I saw water coming out from under the threshold of the temple toward the east (for the temple faced east). The water was coming down from under the south side of the temple, south of the altar. He then brought me out through the north gate and led me around the outside to the outer gate facing east, and the water was trickling from the south side.

As the man went eastward with a measuring line in his hand, he measured off a thousand cubits and then led me through water that was ankle-deep. He measured off another thousand cubits and led me through water that was knee-deep. He measured off another thousand and led me through water that was up to the waist. He measured off another thousand, but now it was a river that I could not cross, because the water had risen and was deep enough to swim in — a river that no one could cross. He asked me, "Son of man, do you see this?"

Then he led me back to the bank of the river. When I arrived there, I saw a great number of trees on each side of the river. He said to me, "This water flows toward the eastern region and goes down into the Arabah, where it enters the Dead Sea. When it empties into the sea, the salty water there becomes fresh. Swarms of living creatures will live wherever the river flows. There will be large numbers of fish, because this water flows there and makes the salt water fresh; so where the river flows everything will live. Fishermen will stand along the shore; from En Gedi to En Eglaim there will be places for spreading nets. The fish will be of many kinds — like the fish of the Mediterranean Sea. But the swamps and marshes will not become fresh; they will be left for salt. Fruit trees of all kinds will grow on both banks of the river. Their leaves will not wither, nor will their fruit fail. Every month they will bear fruit, because the water from the sanctuary flows to them. Their fruit will serve for food and their leaves for healing." (NIV)

There's so much truth written within these verses that gives us a peek into the desires God has for a relationship with us. This is primary for you and me, because if we are going to take others into deeper waters of relationship with the Father, we will have to go there too. We certainly can't take someone where we don't go ourselves.

Wisdom from Past Generations
Every one of God's children ought to be a reproducer.
— Dawson Trotman, evangelist and founder of The Navigators

The first requirement to disciple another is to be a disciple yourself.

Ezekiel was a priest whose name means "God will strengthen." God called him to speak to the Israelite generation that was born in exile, who had never experienced the presence of God in the temple in Jerusalem. The temple had been destroyed and they were living far from any resemblance to the way their fathers lived, with God's presence at the center. Sound like us? Oh, that You, O Lord, would strengthen us to speak to the next generations who have never experienced Your presence at the center of their lives!

Ezekiel was given the gift of visions that spoke to future events for God's chosen people, Israel and Judah. In a vision from God, beginning in Ezekiel 40, God took him to a mountain overlooking the future temple. "The man" has been described as the Angel of the Lord and is even called "Lord," so many people believe this was God Himself in the form of a man. He conducted a tour of all of the details of a new and glorious temple.

As we get to chapter 47, this man led Ezekiel to the entrance of the temple, and water was flowing out from under it. Water is used in many metaphorical ways throughout the Bible, but when it came to the temple, water represents the cleansing power of the presence of God, or the Holy Spirit. The man began to measure off the water in increasing depths, until it was over Ezekiel's head. These are the depths to which the Lord wants to take each person—until he is in over his head, engulfed, and permeated with His presence. This is what Ezekiel was commissioned to tell those born in exile, so that they would remain faithful until the temple, the presence of God, was restored. I believe God is commissioning us to do the same today. He is calling us to go, and to take others who have never experienced Him into a deeper relationship with Him, until we are all in over our heads with the power and the presence of God at the center of our lives.

And just look at the results that are promised: life (abundant and full) wherever the water flows; many more fish of various kinds (other countries, ethnicities, and cultures) coming forth (as disciples); all kinds of trees, bearing all kinds of fruit, will bear every month (Christlikeness will consistently come forth); and that fruit will be food for those who are starving (the Millennials), and leaves (as they grow) will provide healing for those who are wounded and hurting. Now that's worth going after!

In later chapters, we will discuss each measure of depth more specifically in order to help us in the discipleship process. For now, we have a greater understanding of the *people* we will disciple, and the *process* of discipling them. Now we need to find the *pathway* to discipleship: how to get them to the pool so that we can invite them to live in deeper waters with us.

Inside and Outside

We will need to consider again the statistic we learned earlier, that 13 percent of Millennials are still in church and look favorably upon the things of God, while the other 87 percent do not. Since both of these groups need to learn how to walk with God, in deeper relationship with Him, how are we to reach them? Since Jesus was intentional about discipleship, we must do what we saw Him do and be intentional as well. There are three stages through which I see Jesus, and us, intentionally accomplishing our call to discipleship: invite, invest, and imitate.

Wisdom from Past Generations

When you get yourself a man [or a woman], you have more than doubled your ministry. You know why? When you teach your man [or woman], he [or she] sees how it is done, and he [or she] imitates you.
— DAWSON TROTMAN, EVANGELIST AND FOUNDER OF THE NAVIGATORS

Invite

I believe that for both those inside and outside the church, it all starts with an invitation, following the example of Jesus when He invited the disciples to "follow Me." You will have to begin by asking the Father to show you which people He wants you to invite. Keep your spiritual eyes open and alert for people who are open to you and ready to receive the seeds of discipleship.

For some of you, this part is going to be a struggle, because there is no formula for inviting another into discipleship. Jesus invited His disciples to join Him in different ways, and they all came from different walks of life. He offered His invitation to fishermen, tax collectors, the common, the rich, the poor, the educated, and the uneducated. He simply asked the ones that the Father led Him to, and this is what you will do.

Thoughts from Present-Day Leaders

Jesus-shaped spirituality hears Jesus say, "Believe and repent," but the call that resonates most closely in the heart of a disciple is "Follow Me." The command to follow requires that we take a daily journey in the company of other students. It demands that we be lifelong learners and that we commit to constant growth in spiritual maturity. Discipleship is a call to "me," but it is a journey of "we."

— MICHAEL SPENCER, AUTHOR OF *MERE CHURCHIANITY*

Inviting people into your life to disciple them will come naturally, and organically, likely evolving as you spend time developing the relationship. Maybe the Spirit will even tell you during a first meeting to just jump right in and ask. While many of us like structure, I will attempt to give you some ideas, but they must be held loosely before the Lord so that He and you are taking this journey together—and it is not a matter of your just following my instructions. This isn't about the "how" as much as it is about the "Who."

Let's first take a look within the church at the 13 percent who are still favorable toward the church. How will we invite them into discipleship? How will we get them to the pool? Are you wondering why we are starting with reaching the smaller group first? Because the churchgoing Millennial is more open to discipleship, and she also has friends who need to be discipled. You may start out with only one person to disciple, but then that person will tell her friends about it and you will gather more.

First, you must prayerfully ask the Lord to reveal the one or more young women whom you are to disciple. As the Lord reveals those within your church, take some time to get to know them, and then simply ask them if they would allow you to disciple them. And again, if you know only one, but you feel the Lord wants you to disciple more, that one inevitably knows others who may be potential disciples. Be patient and seek the Father's guidance. He'll bring them, because He has been preparing them for you to ask.

If you have ever been canoeing or rafting, you know that if you can't find a decent entry point, you may never get into the lake at all. So it will be with discipleship. You will need to look for places Millennials are and go there so you can help them find their way to the pool.

If there is a college campus nearby or you find that you have a lot of Millennials already attending your church, your women's ministry may want to plan a "fun night" that bridges the generational gaps. You might call it something like "Worlds Apart, Same Heart." Get creative! The program for the night could be for women from each generation to come wearing the clothes from their era; play music from their era; serve a popular food, dessert, or snack from their era; and so on. But they should also share some of what went on in their hearts then and now, including any concerns, insecurities, fears, and more. The goal for the night should be to show that though we as women may all be worlds apart in age and time, our hearts are all the same, giving us a place of commonality. Out of this can flow conversation about the possibility of introducing a discipleship ministry, where the older women disciple the younger. During this event, God may reveal the one you are to disciple. You may even want to have a sign-up for the LIVING DEEPER small-group experiential guides I have written for the next generation. This could be another entry point to getting them to the pool. The possibilities are endless, so get creative, let your imagination fly, and let the Lord direct you to the best ways to reach this next, great generation.

Insights from the Millennials

When I am in my community, I try to see the people I encounter through the eyes of Christ. It makes all the difference in the world.

— KAREN, FROM SOUTH CAROLINA

Here is how God brought me the young women I was to disciple. My son, Cole, began dating a beautiful, talented, smart, and winsome young lady named Kelsey. She began coming to our home with Cole, and she and I became friends. Before I knew it, we were engaging in great conversations, getting to know each other and sharing about where we were in our relationship with God. I knew Kelsey would be the one for my son the day that I met her, but I never knew what a profound impact she would have in my own life and the friendship God would bless us with. I offered myself to her and her friends, to meet as a small group to talk about the things of God. Patiently I prayed for God's timing, and about a year later she asked if we could start a small group. There are five of us who meet on a weekly basis now, and it has been the most joyous, refreshing, and rewarding thing I have been a part of in a long time.

Thoughts from Present-Day Leaders

God actually intended people to be a source of life, a community of support and fellowship, taking care of one another. Genuine fellowship, that sense of having a few people in our lives who really know us, accept us, and love us, can make all the difference in the world.

— CHRIS HODGES, PASTOR OF CHURCH OF THE HIGHLANDS
AND AUTHOR OF FRESH AIR

To reach those outside of the church, the older generation will have to work a little harder. If we are going to reach the other 87 percent, we cannot stay in our safe zones or we will never be where they are. Jesus went to them, and we must do the same. We will have to make an effort to immerse ourselves in places where they might be: colleges, coffeehouses, sports events—both as spectators and as participants—fitness facilities, cooking or art classes, and so on. Find college campuses and partner with what they are already doing; share your intentions with their campus ministries and see where you can plug in or partner together; offer meals once a week for students the school connects you with; or offer your home for holiday celebrations, such as a costume party or a Christmas get-together.

You could construct a website or Facebook page that throws a net out to young women with some common interest. Just as Jesus told the disciples to cast out their nets to become fishers of men, you may need to cast out your net to draw in some disciples through developing a small group. If you think about things you enjoy and then offer that through social networks, college campuses, and so on, you are bound to find yourself with a group of disciples in no time, especially as you pray for God to bring just the right group of young women together. You can offer your house for a supper club or a board game night. You can start a cooking class in your home or develop a hiking or running group. The possibilities truly are endless! Just cast your net and start looking for young women to disciple. God has already prepared them for your encounter. It will be exciting to watch whom He brings across your path!

From there, you will begin to develop a relationship with each of these new disciples. During your times together, share your life and listen as they share their lives with you. See what the Lord develops, and then, as the Spirit leads, invite them to be discipled by you. You may enjoy your time with some but not feel called to disciple them. That's okay. You may even know of someone else who might be a better fit for them and recommend that they join that leader's small group next. Just let God reveal those whom you are to invite to join you. The goal is to develop relationships with others, not faking relationships with them in order to "lure" them into discipleship. These girls can smell "fake" a mile away, and they will run hard and fast in the opposite direction! If you want to disciple the next generations, you will have to become their friend first, and genuinely desire to do so.

Keep in mind that these girls are most likely lost and maybe even disillusioned, skeptical, or resentful of Christianity and the church. Whereas you might use the word *disciple* with the 13 percent within the church, that would not be effective for those outside of it. "Churchy" lingo may be perceived as offensive, pretentious, and indulgent.

Here are some common Christian phrases, as well as new ways to word them so that members of the younger generations can better understand:

- Instead of "Scripture" or "Bible verse," say "a place in the Bible where it says . . ."
- Instead of "believe," say "trust and accept."
- Instead of "Christian," say "follower of Christ."
- Instead of "found the Lord" or "got saved," say "made a decision to follow Christ."
- Instead of "grace," say "God's giving us what we don't deserve."
- Instead of "have a burden," say "I'm concerned."
- Instead of "preach," say "talk about."
- Instead of "repent," say "be sorry about wrongs and turn from them."
- Instead of "salvation" or "saved," say "forgiven of wrongs and given eternal life."
- Instead of "share," say "discuss" or "explain."
- Instead of "sin," say "missing the mark of God's plan for me."
- Instead of "testimony," say "story."
- Instead of "witness," say "tell" or "show."

For those with a negative or adverse attitude toward Christianity and the church, you might say something more like, "I have really enjoyed our time together. I would really like the opportunity to journey through life with you and encourage you as you go. Would you want to do that?" You are simply inviting them into a more frequent and intimate relationship with you. The goal is to meet them where they are without compromising who you are. Above all, be real and be yourself!

Some may ask if this is a manipulative way to reach them with the truth of Christ. I would say, "Absolutely not!" If Jesus Christ is the center of your life, then surely that will be evident to them as you spend time with them. Just as Peter and John could not help but speak about Jesus (see Acts 4:20), when Christ is the consuming portion of your life, you will have a case of the "can't help its" too! Thus, they will be well aware of what you are inviting them into by this point in time. You can even say, "I know God has such a special plan for your life. I sure would like to help you find it and walk with you as we both fulfill God's purposes for our lives."

Also, understand that getting to know each young woman and seeking the Father's direction about which ones to disciple will take some time. Be patient as the Lord develops the relationships and shows you the right time and opportunities. He will go before you and ready them for your invitation. The exciting challenge for you is to walk closer than ever with your heavenly Father, listening for His direction every step of the way. I think you will find that you are being discipled by God in the process, going into ever deeper waters with Him as you disciple and take another person into deeper waters with you. That is just how God works!

Invest

Once God has led you to invite a young woman to join you in discipleship, you must begin to invest yourself in her. Jesus spent most of His time with His disciples. They ate together, prayed together, traveled together, worshipped together, and experienced life together. Throughout all of these times, Jesus was making significant investments in their lives as He encouraged them, spoke truth to them, and loved them in both word and deed.

I heard it once said that when it comes to relationships, you can't take out any withdrawals until you first have made plenty of deposits. There are no withdrawals available without first some deposits being made. Have you ever had people who hardly even know you speak a word of rebuke or criticism to you? For them to think that they have the right to talk to you about such personal things when they haven't even taken time to know you is greatly offensive. Yet Jesus set us a beautiful example by making huge investments in His disciples so that they would then listen to Him — really listen. They knew that Jesus loved them dearly, and so they trusted His leadership when withdrawals eventually became necessary.

Thoughts from Present-Day Leaders

The decision to grow always involves a choice between risk and comfort. This means that to be a follower of Jesus, you must renounce comfort as the ultimate value of your life.

— John Ortberg, PASTOR AND AUTHOR

To make investments as Jesus did requires an availing of your life, time, resources, and energy into the life of another person. It truly is a "laying your life down for your friends" mentality (see John 15:13). It is making yourself fully approachable at any time, day or night. Today, younger generations are suspicious of the "realness" of what they have observed in the church. And yet they are hungry to know the God whom others, who appear to have a walk with Him, have experienced. Letting them into your life to live in intimacy with you is the key. Then, as they open up to you, commit to pray for them. Ask them later how whatever you prayed for is going. It breeds in them a trust that you really are genuine and authentic.

Does this sound hard to you, like it might be a lot of work? The truth is, you are only inviting them to be a part of what you are already doing. They need to see you living out what you say you believe. Take them with you to the grocery store, to the mall, to an assisted-living home, to church, to the doctor's office, or on a lunch date. Let them join you in "doing life together" and invest in them along the way. Find out their favorite foods, color, movie, or flower, and give it to them as a surprise. As you go and do, share the truths of Jesus not only verbally but in your actions, and watch them become transformed by the love of Christ being shown through you! As you invest in them, you are proving yourself trustworthy. You will have to gain their trust first before you are ever going to have the chance to truly speak into their lives. No one will jump into the pool unless they first trust the one who says he or she will catch them. Trust will get them into the pool; truth will take them deeper.

Thoughts from Present-Day Leaders

It is beyond our imaginations what prayer can effect in the earth. When God's name and His renown are the desire of your heart, our prayers for our children, grandchildren, and descendants can be a catalyst that will cause His fame to spread to all the corners of the earth.

— JENNIFER KENNEDY DEAN, SPEAKER AND AUTHOR OF *HEART'S CRY* AND *LEGACY OF PRAYER*

Imitate

Paul exhorted us, "Imitate God, therefore, in everything you do, because you are his dear children. Live a life filled with love, following the example of Christ. He loved us and offered himself as a sacrifice for us, a pleasing aroma to God" (Ephesians 5:1-2, NLT).

The word *imitate* is the Greek word *mimetes*, from which we get our English word *mimic*. It means to imitate or reproduce another's behavior in our lives. God made Himself flesh, dwelling among us (see John 1:1-14), giving us an example to follow. Jesus, the Word made flesh, was the reflection of God for man to imitate. And Jesus modeled discipleship for us as He walked alongside His disciples. He would teach them a particular principle and then show them by example or experience how to apply that to their lives, how it looked in action.

Wisdom from Past Generations

A holy life has a voice. . . . It speaks when the tongue is silent, and is either a constant attraction or a perpetual reproof.
— JOHN HOWARD HINTON, NINETEENTH-CENTURY BAPTIST MINISTER

For example, the first thing He taught His disciples was what we now call the Beatitudes. There He talked about the kingdom of God — and then He went and lived out that kingdom lifestyle of love, sacrifice, and humility before them. Then He sent them out with the assignment to preach the good news and heal the sick, and He later evaluated how it went with them (see Mark 9:28-29). Jesus taught a principle, modeled it before them, and then gave them the opportunity to live it out in their own lives, encouraging them along the way. He offered grace and truth when they failed, and He explained when they didn't understand. He truly gave them, and us, the perfect example to imitate.

Paul wrote, "So I urge you to imitate me . . . just as I imitate Christ" (1 Corinthians 4:16; 11:1, NLT). The first time I read that Scripture, I thought that there was no way I would ever tell someone to imitate me. My first reaction was that Paul must have thought highly of himself if he could say that! But if you look at the writings of Paul, you understand that his heart was not narcissistic at all. He said,

> I don't mean to say that I have already achieved these things or that I have already reached perfection. But I press on to possess that perfection for which Christ Jesus first possessed me. No, dear brothers and sisters, I have not achieved it, but I focus on this one thing: Forgetting the past and looking forward to what lies ahead, I press on to reach the end of the race and receive the heavenly prize for which God, through Christ Jesus, is calling us. (Philippians 3:12-14, NLT)

Insights from the Millennials

I want to be helping repair homes, caring for merchants who lost loved ones, and cleaning up trash for elderly residents. I know it's cliché, but I want to ask the question, "What would Jesus do?" I want to be in the churches that view the community that way.

— KAREN, FROM SOUTH CAROLINA

Paul was saying that he wanted his brothers and sisters in Christ to imitate him in this one way: to make their number one goal the pursuit of knowing Christ and making Him known. This is the same thing you ask those you disciple to imitate in you: not perfection, but pursuing Christ with all that is in you, and striving to look more and more like Him. This is a life worth imitating, holding great accountability for you and great growth in a grace-filled environment for them.

We all want to make a difference in this world, and we all want others to make a difference in us. Has anyone ever really invested in you? Have you ever really invested in another for lifelong change? Jesus told us to store up for ourselves treasures in heaven. The only treasure I know that lasts forever is people.

As you demonstrate the character of Jesus by inviting a young woman into a discipling relationship with you, investing your time, your prayers, your love, and your life into her, imitating your heavenly Father and Jesus Christ as you go, you will not only be winning her trust in you, but you will be helping her win back trust in God and His church. And this kind of trust will cause her to take you by the hand and let you lead her into living deeper with God. That is what coming together to make a real impact in this world is all about.

Thoughts from Present-Day Leaders

Most people in America, when they are exposed to the Christian faith, are not being transformed. They take one step into the door, and the journey ends. They are not being allowed, encouraged, or equipped to love or to think like a Christian. Yet in many ways, a focus on spiritual formation fits what a new generation is really seeking. Transformation is a process, a journey, not a one-time decision.

— DAVID KINNAMAN, AUTHOR OF *unCHRISTIAN*

You are needed to continue the work that Jesus began on this earth—the work of making disciples. We cannot make nearly as much of an impact on this world separately as we could unified and with one common purpose: to make disciples. If each one will reach one, we could unify to help turn our nation back to God! We would not build ourselves a tower of Babel, but rather a nationwide group of temples known as the church that will make the name of Jesus Christ, our Savior, great for His glory and renown. Now that's a mission I want to be a part of! Let's get 'em to the pool so God can take 'em deeper!

Deeper Reflections

1. In which stage of making disciples—invite, invest, or imitate—do you currently find yourself? How are you following God's call within that particular stage?

2. What differences might there be in discipling those inside of the church (13 percent) and those outside of it (87 percent)? To which group do you most relate? Which group do you believe God is calling you to reach out to?

3. Brainstorm some ideas for how you might reach out to those in younger generations—both inside and outside of the church. What practical things can you do to bridge the generational gap?

4. Which of the traditionally "Christian" phrases do you most often use in your everyday language? How hard would it be to begin to "speak the language" of the younger generations? What do you find most challenging about this? Or do you find it challenging at all?

5. The chapter asks, "Has anyone ever really invested in you? Have you ever really invested in another for lifelong change?" Think about your answers to these questions. What difference did another person's investment make in your life? How can you "pay it forward" to the next generation of young women?

3

ankle-deep

All other things are incidental to the supreme task of winning a man or woman to Jesus Christ and then helping him or her to go on.

— DAWSON TROTMAN

Think about the first thing you do when you go to the pool. You put your towel on the lounge chair, walk over to the edge of the pool, and stick your toes into the water to see whether it is cold or not. I guess we all do that to know just how slowly we will have to get into the pool in order to acclimate ourselves to the temperature. Funny how it is almost always cold, but we still have to check it out and determine this for ourselves! (It's kind of like when someone smells something bad and then tells you to smell it for yourself. Even though he just told you it smelled disgusting, you will still take a sniff—we just have to experience things for ourselves.) Finally, after we have stepped in and our toes are accustomed to the cold water, we find ourselves ready to step on in a little bit deeper.

This is what disciples at ankle-deep are all about. They will be testing the waters to see whether or not you are real, whether the Christian walk is real, and whether what they desire can become a reality for them. The answers they find at ankle-deep will determine whether they choose to live deeper in relationship with God and with others. Ankle-deep will also be the depth where they get acclimated to what it truly means to have a relationship with God.

When I had my first meeting with the young women I was

going to disciple, they were quiet, closed, unsure, and questioning. They were not sure what to do with me, and I was not sure what to do with them! They were trying to see if I was "real," without any facade or veneer. They wanted to see if I would be honest with them about myself, or if I would think more highly of myself than reality would reveal. My openness determined how open they would become with me.

Who They Are

Let's define those who might be considered ankle-deep.

- They may not know Jesus as Savior and Lord—yet. Some may have never even heard the good news nor accepted Jesus Christ, and you will get the incredible privilege of leading them to salvation in Him! Salvation will be their first step into an ankle-deep relationship with Christ.

Insights from the Millennials

I accepted Christ, but I have never been discipled.

— DEE, FROM SOUTH CAROLINA

- They may be new in their faith in Jesus Christ. Some may be brand-new believers who are just beginning this journey of walking with God, and you get to help them know how to do that.

Insights from the Millennials

True discipling didn't begin until twenty years after I was saved— very sad.

— AMY, FROM GEORGIA

- They may have been Christians for a long time, but they have never been discipled. Let me explain a few things about this group: I will never forget when I was teaching a college and career small group at my church. I threw out a question about what they had found the most difficult in their Christian experience. One young man raised his hand and said, "I realized I needed Jesus as my Savior and Lord, asked Him into my heart, and got baptized; but after that, no one told me what was next and I've just been stuck ever since and haven't grown at all because no one showed me how." You will be surprised to find that many people have come to know Jesus Christ as Savior, have been baptized, joined the local church, and had others come by and give them a handshake of welcome into the family of God; but then they were left with no idea of what happens after that. They have no clue how to grow their faith—they may not even know that they need to grow. My heart breaks for those who have come to the ankle-deep waters but have been stuck at the side of the pool with no one to reach out and help them go deeper.

Wisdom from Past Generations

Being a Christian is more than just an instantaneous conversion — it is a daily process whereby you grow to be more and more like Christ.

— BILLY GRAHAM, EVANGELIST

Where They Are Skeptical

Most of those who begin to be discipled by you will be skeptical of both you and God. They have seen too much hypocrisy in their lifetimes, and they are uncertain of anyone who says she is not a hypocrite. They carry a lot of doubt that must be overcome with truth. They will be looking to see if your walk matches your talk. They don't want you to be perfect—just real and truly striving to be the person you say you want to become. Their desire is to see pursuit, not perfection.

Leery

They have lost all trust in relationships. They have not only been inundated with media influences that show manipulation, abuse, and deception, but they have also personally experienced bad relationships. Because of this, relationships have been tainted and the hope for genuine ones feels unattainable. They need you to be trustworthy, and you will have to earn their trust because they won't easily give it.

Eager

For the most part, you will find that these new disciples *want* to learn from you. They have seen life conducted so badly in the past that they want to seek ways to do things better in their future. You will find that they are enthusiastic about meeting together and interacting with you in a question-and-discussion dialogue as they seek answers to their problems and issues.

Self-Assured

This generation is often misunderstood to be cocky, even arrogant. The reality is that they have been overloaded with information and are very knowledgeable about many subjects. Thus they have an opinion on just about everything! They are confident that they make a difference in this world simply because they know enough to make it happen. Instead of cutting them off at the knees to humble them, it is important to channel that confidence into productivity so they can put what they know into practice. It is here that they will both be humbled and find that they need to revisit some of their belief systems. They will need affirmation that their belief systems are reliable and align with the Word of God. As a discipler, you will want to take them on a journey to be confident not in their intellect but in their relationship with God through Jesus.

Thoughts from Present-Day Leaders

I find it interesting that we tend to base our beliefs regarding God's goodness and love on the nature of the surprises He gives us. As long as His surprises are happy ones like birthday parties, we remain confident and secure: He really is good! He evidently loves me a lot! But all too often unwanted surprises have a way of turning our theology upside down.

—TRAVIS COTTRELL, WORSHIP LEADER AND AUTHOR OF *SURPRISED BY WORSHIP*

Unaware

They have never looked at life's experiences as a process for growth. To look at life as a classroom where God is preparing them for what is to come is a foreign concept to them. Experiencing God together and walking and talking with another person throughout the day will be equally new to them. They will need much guidance and grace as they learn what this is like and how to begin this new intimacy in relationship.

Unlearned

For the most part, though they're saturated with information, how to process and put the information into practice is difficult for them. They are many times confused by the extreme differences in the teaching of our culture and the teachings of Jesus, and they can have a difficult time separating them when Christians exemplify both in their lifestyles. They have a strong disdain for hypocrisy and will not allow that to become who they are. As a result, from observing us, they often look at the Scriptures as "suggestions" rather than "imperatives." Taking time to educate them on the teachings of Jesus and His heart behind His teaching, as well as how to apply that to their lives, is an essential element in the discipling process.

How to Respond

Those who are ankle-deep may have a lot of questions and very few answers. For the first time, they are testing the waters with you, and maybe even with God. They will be looking to you to see whether this is worth going a little deeper or not. They may not understand much and will need your guidance on what this thing called the "Christian life" is all about. So as you begin this discipleship journey with them, your number one goal is to *enlighten*.

Enlighten

In Ephesians 1:18, Paul was writing to the church in Ephesus and said, "I pray that the eyes of your heart may be enlightened" (NIV). The word *enlightened* is the Greek word *photizo*, from which we get our word *photo*, and means "to shine light on; to illuminate; to instruct, inform, and give understanding to."

Inspiration from God's Word

No one lights a lamp, then hides it in a drawer. It's put on a lamp stand so those entering the room have light to see where they're going.

— LUKE 11:33

Paul wanted to bring the Christians at Ephesus to a full understanding of the great riches offered them by faith in Christ Jesus. You will get the opportunity to do the same. Many believers, new and old alike, do not even know what was afforded them when they accepted Jesus Christ as Savior and Lord. Through discipleship, you will get the beautiful privilege and joy of shining light on spiritual things that were once dark for her. When Jesus said that we are the light of the world, He meant for us to illuminate those around us with the love and life He offered through His life, death, and resurrection.

As a discipler, you can enlighten disciples in six very specific areas.

1. Enlighten Them to Truth

Because Millennials are inundated with all kinds of information, it can leave them uncertain about what is really true. They will need to be taught what the Bible says so that they will have no doubt. We need to shed light on three things that Paul specifically wanted others to understand. First, Paul wanted them to "know what is the hope of his [Jesus'] calling" (Ephesians 1:18, KJV). We must help others know the confidence of an intimate relationship with God through Jesus Christ that starts at salvation and goes on into eternity. The word *hope* means "a confident expectancy." What confidences do we have through salvation? We have confidence of forgiveness; we have confidence of unconditional and unfailing love; we have confidence that our salvation is secure; and we have confidence that He is always with us.

One of your greatest callings is to help Millennials understand that God's deep love for them caused Him to invite them back into an intimate relationship with Him by sending His only Son for them. This is the greatest sacrificial love story of all time. The fact that it is a love that no one can alter or take away gives them the confidence they need to live free from the penalty and guilt of sin, free from the rejection and scorn of others, and free to become all that God originally created them to be. This great love will also cause them to sacrifice and give their lives freely to Him.

Second, Paul wanted them to know "the riches of the glory of his inheritance in the saints" (Ephesians 1:18, KJV). Followers of Jesus must know all that they inherit as a daughter—a princess—of the King of kings. That word *riches* means "to be filled with abundance." In John 10:10, Jesus said, "I came so they can have real and eternal life, more and better life than they ever dreamed of." The word *life* is the Greek word *zoe* and means "vibrancy, animation, excitement." Disciples of Jesus Christ get to experience life to its fullest! They get to walk with God, free from worries, shame, and bondage to sin, and free to love others, to surrender to the leading and prompting of the Holy Spirit, and to talk with God twenty-four hours a day, seven days a week! Paul also wanted them to know the beauty of being an heir. As a child of God, you receive an inheritance when Jesus returns and establishes His kingdom. You get a lavish, magnificent portion of it! In addition, you are no longer called by any label, but you are called a saint. A new disciple must realize the truth that they receive both a new name and abundant life now, while the promise of a blessed allotment as a daughter of God is yet to come. They need to know God as Father.

> **Wisdom from Past Generations**
>
> Preaching is to much avail, but practice is far more effective. A godly life is the strongest argument you can offer a skeptic.
>
> — HOSEA BALLOU, NINETEENTH-CENTURY THEOLOGIAN AND WRITER

Finally, Paul desired for them to know the "incomparably great power for us who believe" (Ephesians 1:19, NIV). New disciples need to know that they are not alone. They have been given an all-surpassing great power! That word *power* is the Greek word *dunamis*, which is where we get our word *dynamite*, and it means "an inherent strength that resides from within to be moral, perform miracles, and to influence based on the resources given by a host or army."

God is known as the Lord of hosts, and He has given us power through the Holy Spirit deposited within us at salvation, as well as the resources of His army of angels to empower us to be all He created us to be. John tells us that the Holy Spirit is present to be our Helper, to come alongside of us to guide us, remind us, and counsel us on the ways of God. In Ephesians 1:13-14, Paul said that the Holy Spirit was deposited in us as yet another gift of our inheritance, as our promised guarantee of what awaits us. The Holy Spirit is called a "seal," because in those days, a wax seal was placed on items to show a final transaction, ownership, and a security that can never be taken away. God gave you the Holy Spirit to say that your salvation is a "done deal"—that you are completely His and He is completely yours, and nothing and no one can ever take that away. Your disciples need to know God as Holy Spirit. Enlightening them to the truth of the Trinity overcomes their doubt and gives them the confidence they've been searching for. For some of you, this is a great reminder. God has provided you all of the power you need to disciple.

2. Enlighten Them to Authentic Relationships

Without trust, no one would believe what another person says. Because this generation is so untrusting, you will have to both prove your trustworthiness and earn their trust. As a discipler, the surest way to build trust in your relationships is by your actions. Jesus earned the trust of His disciples by constantly proving His love and commitment to them by His actions. As you begin to disciple another person, it is vitally important that you build a foundation of choices and deeds that prove you trustworthy. Not repeating a matter she shared with you in confidence, keeping your promises, pointing her to Christ to meet her needs, and faithfully being available for her when she needs you are great ways to earn her unwavering trust. Once this is established, she will allow you to walk with her through difficult situations that help her grow in Christlikeness.

Wisdom from Past Generations

In the New Testament, the word disciple does not appear except in the Gospels and in Acts. It is never the case of a "pupil" who receives instruction from a master, but always of someone who shares a close and definitive relationship with one person.

— XAVIER LÉON-DUFOUR, FRENCH JESUIT

As I am building my relationship with these girls, I find that one of the ways that really breeds trust in our relationship is when I say that I will pray for them and then I actually do it! Many times I text them before whatever they had asked me to pray for occurs, and I let them know that the Holy Spirit reminded me to pray for them. It means so much to them and encourages them to trust in the authenticity of my deep caring and love.

3. Enlighten Them to Grace

In their eagerness to learn how to walk with God and become all that He made them to become, they will find that life is filled with both ups and downs, successes and failures. This is where much grace and understanding come on your part. Jesus came with grace and truth (see John 1:14). Many times, we approach people with truth only, meaning that we tell them what the Bible commands but not the grace it offers as they learn to walk that truth out in life. Sometimes reminding another of God's precepts and commands comes across so harsh that new believers are overwhelmed with the pressure to perform and the fear of punishment when they fail. It can make new disciples become legalistic rule followers, while missing the goal of relationship with God through Christ Jesus.

On the other hand, we can approach people with so much grace that we give them permission to develop a relativistic mentality. This causes them to presume upon the grace of God, walking in the freedom to live however they want, because they believe God's grace will cover it all. This free-rein mentality makes them feel they have a license to do and be however they want because God will simply forgive them. They misunderstand God's design and goal for them and the protective purposes of the parameters set forth in His Word. Jesus showed us that both grace and truth are needed in all of our relationships, but certainly, they are needed in the relationship between you and new disciples of Christ. They need to know God's boundaries, laid out in His Word, as well as the reasons He gave them. They also need to know that at their salvation they were given the Holy Spirit to live inside of them to help them remain within those boundaries. But they must also have the assurance that in their attempts to surrender to the Lord and live for Him, God will offer them grace when they fall. Grace and truth provide them the ability to learn through the process.

When I taught my children how to ride a bike, I started with the fundamentals of bike riding. As they tried to ride, they would have times of success and failure. When they fell, I would dust their britches off and put them back on the bike to try again. New disciples of Jesus need to know that God will lovingly treat them the same way—and so will you.

Wisdom from Past Generations

The man that believes will obey; failure to obey is living proof that there is no true faith present.

— A. W. Tozer, twentieth-century pastor, preacher, and author

4. Enlighten Them to Dependence

Part of the Christian life is learning how to grow from living totally independent of God, relying on self, to living totally dependent on God, relying on Him. Jesus said that if any man (or woman) were to follow Him, he would have to deny himself, take up his cross, and follow Him. Part of discipleship is helping disciples learn how to deny what they want, crucify their fleshly desires, and surrender to the leadership of Jesus through willing obedience. Relying not on the flesh but completely on Jesus will be new, risky, and fearful. Take your girls through a ropes course, play "trust fall" with them, or even take them skydiving. That will give them a physical understanding of this spiritual abandonment to Christ.

> **Wisdom from Past Generations**
> Salvation is free, but discipleship will cost you your life.
> — DIETRICH BONHOEFFER, TWENTIETH-CENTURY MARTYR

5. Enlighten Them to Opportunities for Growth

Most new disciples will talk about their current situation as something that has happened and cannot be altered, as if now it is just a matter of figuring out how to fix the current circumstance. It is going to be a joy to help these disciples learn to change their perspective of life's circumstances from fixing to faith, from griping to growth. You will be helping them understand that while they are after relief, God is after a relationship with them. He is using life to be their teacher, and He wants them to begin to ask with each situation that arises, *What are You up to this time, Lord? What do You want to teach me?* This will become a launching pad for them to interact with God throughout their day, and to embrace the fact that truly all things do work together for good to those who love the Lord and are called according to His purpose (see Romans 8:28).

6. Enlighten Them to Biblical Lenses

Putting on a new set of lenses is crucial to a disciple. In Ephesians 1:18, the word *eye* is the Greek word *ophthalmos*, from which we get our word *ophthalmology*, a branch of medicine that treats the deep things within the eye. God wants to change the way we see things. He wants us to see the deeper, spiritual things hidden beneath our physical eyesight. There are many ways in which to view the world, but God desires for us to have a biblical worldview. He wants us to be able to look at the world through the lenses of what His Word says about that particular part of the world we are viewing. He wants us to start asking, *What does God's Word say about that?* Taking this stance will certainly encourage the new disciple to search God's Word for an answer, ask the Holy Spirit to reveal truth, and even begin some dialogue with you to help in the search. Once that truth is found, it serves as a truth that can be trusted without any doubt. Confidence in Scripture, as well as in the God of the Scriptures, begins to grow and strengthen the heart of this new disciple of Jesus Christ.

Thoughts from Present-Day Leaders

Sending young people into the world without a biblical worldview is like sending a ball player onto the field without a playbook.

— Voddie Baucham, pastor and author

As my relationship with Kelsey grew, it was amazing to watch all that God was showing her as she walked into the waters with Jesus. Her honesty, humility, and teachable spirit inspired me to stay that way and continue walking deeper with God as well. We began to trust one another. We even hit a few bumps in the road. But the deep desire to understand and really relate to one another forged a great bond between the two of us. I pray you find this with the ones you disciple, as well!

If you will recall from the verses in Ezekiel 47, the first place the Spirit led measured ankle-deep. The word *ankle* is the Hebrew word *ephec*, and means "to disappear; to cease; to be clean gone; at an end; no further; at the ankles." Over the course of time, as you have been discipling in ankle-deep waters, there has been much of "self" that has come to an end. Fleshly thoughts, habits, misunderstandings, confusion, skepticism, and cynicism are beginning to cease. Self-sufficiency has begun to disappear. When this occurs, a disciple can no longer take one step further without seeing things from a spiritual and biblical perspective.

This is where Paul's heart was when he wrote to the Christians at Ephesus. His desire was for Christians to know the truth of who they are and what their lives should look like as a result of that discovery.

He desired this truth to take them to the end of themselves and become completely and solely confident in and dependent on the Lord Jesus Christ.

In 1 Corinthians 16:8-9, Paul even said, "For the present, I'm staying right here in Ephesus. A huge door of opportunity for good work has opened up here." Now, get this. The word *Ephesus* in this passage is from the Hebrew word *ephec*, or "ankle." May I suggest to you that Paul was staying on with the Christians who were ankle-deep, coming to the end of themselves completely, until the Holy Spirit came to empower them. He knew this would be a doorway to some effective and life-changing work that was about to take place in these people.

You have become like Paul by staying with this ankle-deep disciple as she has begun the journey of coming to the end of herself so that God can do a mighty work in and through her. Ankle-deep discipleship is an exciting experience as you begin to watch her grow. Continue to let God use you to enlighten her to truth. You will begin to see more of a reliance on God than on self. You will see the truth take over her doubt. Your friendship with her will grow in ruthless trust. And the beautiful surrender of her life to the leadership of the Holy Spirit will emerge. She has tested the waters and found them true, and at this place, she is now ready to venture out into deeper waters with you and God.

Deeper Reflections

1. Do you know anyone who is "ankle-deep" in the discipleship process? What is her story? What practical things can you do to reach her?

2. Where are you personally when it comes to the description of an "ankle-deep Christian"? Which of the defining characteristics — skeptical, leery, eager, self-assured, unaware,

or unlearned — best describe you? What challenges you to move on with God in living deeper with Him?

3. The younger generations need to be enlightened to various aspects of the Christian faith. Which of these aspects might you find most challenging to share? Why? What can you do to more effectively disciple a member of the younger generation in this way?

4. What does it mean to you to have an "authentic relationship" with someone? What characteristics are most important in such a relationship? How can you cultivate these characteristics with the person whom you are discipling?

5. How can you grow the person you are discipling past ankle-deep waters and into a deeper walk with God?

4

knee-deep

Jesus of Nazareth always comes asking disciples to follow Him — not merely "accept Him," not merely "believe in Him," not merely "worship Him," but to follow Him: one either follows Christ, or one does not. There is no compartmentalization of the faith, no realm, no sphere, no business, no politic in which the lordship of Christ will be excluded. We either make Him Lord of all lords, or we deny Him as Lord of any.

— LEE CAMP

For several years, as God was preparing me for what He had called me to, I was privileged to be a minister to children in several churches. One of the things that the Lord reminded me of early on was the value of squatting down and opening my arms to children. How many children have you seen run up and hug around a set of knees and then look up in a panic to find that the person attached to those knees was not their mama? All knees may look the same, but all faces do not. It's when I bent down that the children could truly see my face and embrace me for who I was.

Inspiration from God's Word
Those who look to him are radiant.

— PSALM 34:5, NIV

As a disciple moves from ankle-deep to knee-deep, she will begin to bend her knees as she bows her heart to more of the lordship of Jesus Christ. She begins to lose herself in all of who He is, letting go of the past and finding healing in His open arms that are never ever closed to us. The more we kneel, the more of His face we see, and the more others see His face on us. Psalm 27:8 says, "My heart says of you, 'Seek his face!' Your face, LORD, I will seek" (NIV). We may have sought a lot of things that we thought would fill us, but once we look into the face of and embrace the only One who can heal us, we will find wholeness in our hearts.

Who They Are

Let's define those who might be considered knee-deep:

- They know Jesus as Savior and are growing under His lordship. What I mean by lordship is that they are beginning to trust God enough to let Him lead; they are giving over more control and allowing Him to be master of their lives, choosing to let Him drive while they ride in the passenger's seat. They are becoming obedient to His precepts, and His leading is becoming a part of their everyday lives.
- They are believers who are recognizing fleshly, carnal areas in their lives that need to be eradicated. God is beginning to grow larger in their lives, pushing all selfish, independent ways and mind-sets out of the way to make room for more of Himself.
- They are believers who are taking a new view of their circumstances and understanding spiritual warfare for the first time. As their lives unfold before them, they become more aware that life is not mere "happenstance," but rather God growing them while the Enemy seeks to destroy them.

Wisdom from Past Generations

There is no neutral ground in the universe; every square inch, every split second is claimed by God and counterclaimed by Satan.

— C. S. LEWIS, TWENTIETH-CENTURY PHILOSOPHER AND AUTHOR

Where They Are

Knee-deep disciples are less guarded. As you have exhibited much grace and they have found you trustworthy, authentic, and true, they have begun to let their guard down with both you and God. They will trust you to lead them and will make themselves available to wherever the Lord wants to take them next. As they begin living in deeper waters with God, you will be there to help them understand more and more of the truth revealed. Never forget: Grace gets them into the water, and truth takes them deeper.

Knee-deep disciples are more communicative. They begin to open up and have more genuine and real dialogue with you, since you have proved and continue to prove yourself trustworthy. They want to learn more and more from you, but they also want you to hear from *them*. They need a listening ear. Some may want to process what they are learning out in the open with you, while others will process it internally and then come to you for affirmation that they are headed in the right direction. There will also be things that they don't quite understand, for which they'll need your wisdom and insight.

Knee-deep disciples are less excited. Each time you meet together, there is less excitement, sometimes because of the monotony and sometimes because they are being challenged and are beginning to realize that there is so much they don't know or understand. This can almost be too much for them, and they may grow a little weary. Around this time, Satan also loves to try to draw them into complacency. He sees his grip on their lives loosening each time you get together. Do not become overly concerned. It is all part of the discipleship process and will not last forever. God wants both them and you to learn to persevere. He is using this to make both of you stronger, so press through and press in to hear more of what the Lord wants to do in your time together.

At one point in my journey with my discipleship small group, there came a lull. It was almost like a comfortableness that was good and yet it had the potential to slip over into complacency. We all had to "re-up" and refocus our hearts toward what God was up to with the group. We moved through it, and God blessed our perseverance.

Knee-deep disciples are less assured in themselves. Many will begin to realize that while they know a lot, they still have a lot to learn. While they will remain ready to roll up their sleeves and take action to change their world, a newfound humility will grow as they realize that they have just scratched the surface of their relationship with Jesus Christ. They will also begin to understand the warfare in the Spirit that they may have not otherwise understood, much less learned how to fight.

Thoughts from Present-Day Leaders

Like a skilled and masterful thief, the enemy daily steals the joy, strength and passion of Christians, and many do not even realize what they have lost or how much.

— FRANCIS FRANGIPANE, PASTOR AND AUTHOR OF *THE THREE BATTLEGROUNDS*

Knee-deep disciples are inexperienced. Many of them have operated from their flesh and their self. Living with Jesus being the boss of their lives is new for them. They, more than likely, have not been taught how to put on the armor of God and overcome the Enemy as they seek to live in relationship with Jesus. They are fighting to understand who they are and who God created them to be. As they begin to understand who God says they are, the Enemy will do his best to keep them from finding and walking in that freeing truth. As a discipler, you must stay alert to the ways Satan will seek to come against the group you disciple.

Inspiration from God's Word

The Devil is poised to pounce, and would like nothing better than to catch you napping. Keep your guard up.

— 1 Peter 5:8

Knee-deep disciples are inadequate. They will feel incredibly inadequate as they seek to determine their true identity and live that out. This truly is a great place for them and you to be because it requires total dependence on Christ. They will feel equally inadequate in understanding the schemes of the Enemy and how to combat him. The good news is that in those feelings of inadequacy, they will find a strengthened faith as God proves to be adequate for them. In their weakness, He will prove strong, and a confidence in Him as they've never known will be forged deep within. With that confidence, they will begin to turn this world upside down for the cause of Jesus Christ.

How to Respond to Those Who Are Knee-Deep

These who are knee-deep are growing and learning, while going from confidence in their intelligence to realizing that they still have much to learn. As they trust you to take them into deeper waters with you, they will need you to contribute to this process and the progress God is making in their lives. At this stage in the discipleship journey, the greatest offering you can make is to *encourage* them.

Inspiration from God's Word

Let us not become weary in doing good, for at the proper time we will reap a harvest if we do not give up.

— Galatians 6:9, niv

Hebrews 3:13 says, "Encourage one another daily, as long as it is called 'Today'" (niv). The word *encourage* is *parakaleo*, from which we get our word *paraclete*. It means "to call to one's side; to admonish; to beg; to console; to give strength; to instruct." This verb is similar to the word used as a noun in John 14:16-17, when Jesus said, "And I will ask the Father, and he will give you another advocate to help you and be with you forever—the Spirit of truth" (NIV). The word *advocate* here is *parakletas*, and it means "the one called to another's side, to lead into deeper truth and to divinely strengthen." What an incredible thought—that the Lord would entrust *you* to be filled with the Holy Spirit and allow the Spirit to live through you to come alongside another disciple to exhort, plead, comfort, fortify, and teach her! That's a humbling privilege, filled with great responsibility. Just know that God sees you and is confident in your surrender to His guidance in your life. He knows you have what it takes to disciple another of His beloved children.

So let's consider this question: *For what specific things will knee-deep disciples need encouragement?*

Encourage them when relationships get hard. As they grow in their relationship with both God and others, they will find times of struggle. Maybe God will seem silent or distant. Maybe He will not answer a prayer in just the way they desire. Maybe a conflict will arise within their earthly relationships. Maybe the two of you will disagree. Whatever the situation, there will be a temptation to doubt or, at the very least, question. One of the first places Satan loves to attack us is in the area of relationships, because he knows how relationally we were created. You will be greatly needed to encourage them to press through, trusting that God does work all things together for His good (see Romans 8:28). They will need encouragement to keep going, trusting that God is going to use this to grow their faith.

At one point or another, I have had a difference of opinion and response to a particular situation than some of the girls in my small group. The beauty has been that even though we may be different, and even though we see things differently, we've been able to look past those differences and try to see and understand the differences. We can even consider the differences and take them before the Lord. The outcome has, so far, been great growth for all of us when our attitudes are open to the perspective of each other.

As I am writing this, I am sitting at the airport. I had a perfectly smooth flight, but I have certainly had some pretty turbulent ones, as well. I have no worries when the ride is smooth, but boy, does my anxiety level rise when things start getting really bouncy! I think that is what happens to a disciple when it comes to relationships. When things are going well with God and others, there are no worries (and sometimes complacency sets in and no growth occurs). However, when relationships begin to get a little turbulent, these new disciples tend to get anxious, and they are tempted to either control in order to fix (go and knock on the cockpit door), or walk away (get off the plane altogether). Disciples will need you to encourage them when relational turbulence occurs.

Encourage them when they doubt who God is. When hard times in life come, many disciples will be tempted, as was Eve, to question God and His intentions for them. *Is God really good? Are His intentions for me really good? Is God holding out on me? Does He really even care?* These may all be questions that arise when troubles come. Without your encouragement, as we also saw with Eve, this doubting of God will lead to an open place for the Enemy to deceive and turn doubt to deception. This inevitably leads to disobedience. With your encouragement, disciples will be made aware of what is happening and lean on you to help them find their way back to the true heart of God and His unfailing love for them.

Encourage them when Satan wages war. As they begin to walk closer to God, they are going to begin to recognize the assault that the Enemy is launching against them. Whereas before they may have looked at it as "just life," they are now realizing that there is an Enemy of their souls who wants to destroy them and their walk with God, and the life that they were created to enjoy. They will see his relentless attempts to snuff out the light of Christ in their lives, seeking to take back any ground that has already been made.

Wisdom from Past Generations

Satan has in fact a plan against the saints of the Most High, which is to wear them out.

— WATCHMAN NEE, TWENTIETH-CENTURY CHINESE AUTHOR AND CHURCH LEADER

It reminds me of a punching bag that I once had as a kid. You know, the tall, blow-up kind. It had sand or some other kind of weight in the bottom, so that when you punched it down, it would always pop right back up. It could take the hardest hits but still pop back up every time. This is what disciples will feel like as they begin to learn how to take the punches of the Enemy and then pop back up. They will need to know that God is with them and has given them the weapons of warfare to overcome their Enemy. And they will need you to give them the courage to fight, to put on and apply the armor of God, and to continue to learn how to fight Satan well. They will need you to remind their souls that they are more than conquerors through Jesus Christ (see Romans 8:37), and that no weapon formed against them will ever prosper (see Isaiah 54:17). They will need reminding that they are pressed but not crushed, persecuted but not abandoned, struck down but not destroyed (see 2 Corinthians 4:8-9). We as disciples of Jesus pop right back up! They will need to talk this out with you often and watch you diligently as you show them how to do this by your example.

Encourage them when they struggle with learning and living out their new identity. As disciples move into knee-deep water, they will begin to learn more and more about who God says they are, which is most often contrary to what the world and others have told them. Satan also tries to throw in his lies to set confusion in their hearts and minds, to further obstruct the truth and their finding the freedom to live in this newfound identity.

Wisdom from Past Generations

Moses spent forty years in the king's palace thinking he was a somebody, then lived forty more years in the wilderness finding out that without God he was a nobody, and finally spent forty more years discovering how a nobody with God can be a somebody.

— DWIGHT L. MOODY, NINETEENTH-CENTURY AMERICAN EVANGELIST AND PUBLISHER

I remember the very first time I sought to wear high heels. I had never worn a pair before, and while I liked the fit and the new look, it took some getting used to. I found myself quickly going back to an older pair of shoes that was not too high and much more comfortable to me. When it comes to our new identity in Christ, it will be much like putting on a new pair of high heels that are just the perfect fit and look for us. But while we try to adjust to this newly acquired covering, we will be tempted to go back to our old, more comfortable way of life when circumstances arise that threaten who we are. We will seek to go back to our old identity to cope, respond, and fix life's situations instead of clinging to the truth of who we are and learning to let God work out this newness within. You will need to be constantly available for your disciples to talk with you about this, as they seek direction from you and watch you practice this in your own life.

Wisdom from Past Generations

Well done is better than well said.

— BENJAMIN FRANKLIN, FOUNDING FATHER OF THE UNITED STATES

Of all the parts of the body, the knee is the strongest. With its intricate details, it forms a complex mechanism that can carry much weight and is still flexible enough to withstand many twists and turns. It is no wonder that the next measure of depth the Spirit takes disciples to is knee-deep. They will have to learn how to be strong and how to respond when life takes them on twists and turns. The knee is also the part that attaches the thigh to the lower leg. In Scripture, the thigh represents covenant, or promise, while the leg represents action. As disciples move from ankle-deep to knee-deep, they will begin to better understand the powerful promises that a covenant relationship with God brings, and then they will learn how to live in light of those promises as they walk out their own faith.

> **Wisdom from Past Generations**
> Fairest and best is she whose clothing is humility.
> — JAMES MONTGOMERY, NINETEENTH-CENTURY BRITISH EDITOR, HYMN WRITER, AND POET

Although the knee represents strength, it first represents humility. The word *knee* in the Hebrew is *berek* and means "to kneel; to bless God as an act of adoration." Throughout Scripture, men fell to their knees when entering the presence of almighty God. Even today, people kneel when royalty passes by. To bend the knee shows deep respect, honor, and courtesy to one who is superior. It is as if to say, *I recognize and acknowledge who you are and who I am in light of who you are.* It also shows great allegiance to a person; it expresses a sense of loyalty. It is like saying, *I bend my knee and I bow my head to your authority over my life.*

Finally, bending the knee is the ultimate expression of worship. In John 4:23-24, Jesus said that the true worshippers the Father seeks must worship Him in spirit and in truth. The word *worship* here is *proskyneo,* and it means "to fall upon the knees as an expression of profound reverence." The word *spirit* here is *pneuma*, and it means "soul: mind, emotions, and will," while *truth* is *aletheia* and means "reality; fact; personal honesty and authenticity." Worship is the act of humbly recognizing our nothingness apart from God and His grace, and responding with a life that says, "I know to whom I give my allegiance, and I mean it with all of my heart." When engaging in praise and worship to the Lord through music, the disciple says, "I know what I am singing, and I mean it with all of my heart."

Psalm 95:6 says, "So come, let us worship: bow before him, on your knees before GOD, who made us!"

Isaiah 45:23 says,

I am GOD,
the only God there is, the one and only.
I promise in my own name:
Every word out of my mouth does what it says.
I never take back what I say.
Everyone is going to end up kneeling before me.
Everyone is going to end up saying of me,
"Yes! Salvation and strength are in God!"

This links to Philippians 2:9-11, which says that "because of [Jesus'] obedience, God lifted him high and honored him far beyond anyone or anything, ever, so that all created beings in heaven and on earth—even those long ago dead and buried—will bow in worship before this Jesus Christ, and call out in praise that he is the Master of all, to the glorious honor of God the Father." It also correlates to Romans 14:11, which says the same thing.

Wisdom from Past Generations

Example is not the main thing in influencing others. It is the only thing.

— ALBERT SCHWEITZER, TWENTIETH-CENTURY GERMAN THEOLOGIAN

Based on what we have learned, you will lead knee-deep disciples to learn humble strength. They will recognize their nothingness apart from Jesus Christ, and as they bow to His authority in and through their lives, they will live with a Spirit-filled strength and power that can overcome anything the Enemy could hurl their direction. They will walk in who God says they are with great confidence and security, not in themselves but in the One who has been given His rightful place as Lord. And the best way you can encourage this in their lives is for you to live it out before them: "So don't sit around on your hands! No more dragging your feet! Clear the path for long-distance runners so no one will trip and fall, so no one will step in a hole and sprain an ankle. Help each other out. And run for it!" (Hebrews 12:12-13).

My husband, Dale, was traveling to speak in Florida. As he settled into his seat on an airplane, hoping to rest up and prepare for ministering the next day, a gentleman sat beside him and began to ask Dale where he was going and what he was doing when he got there. After Dale shared a bit, he asked the young man the same thing. He shared with Dale that he was a physical therapist and worked with victims of car accidents who were left paralyzed. His goal was to help them walk again, but for many, the journey was painful. Dale asked the therapist what motivated them to walk, and not give up in the pain and discouragement. Immediately he responded, "Two simple things: They remember what it was like to walk, and they see other people walking."

As one who is discipling others, you can give them great encouragement by two simple things: Remember what it was like when you walked so closely to the Lord and then walk that way before them. As they see you walking, they will want to walk right alongside you into living in even deeper waters with the Father.

Deeper Reflections

1. Do you know anyone who is "knee-deep" in the discipleship process? What is her story? What practical things can you do to reach her?

2. Where are you when it comes to the description of a "knee-deep Christian"? Which of the defining characteristics—less guarded,

more communicative, less excited, less self-assured, inexperienced, or inadequate — best describes you? What ultimately helps you move on to the next stage?

3. Are the young women whom you are discipling through this stage facing any discouragement in their Christian walk? If so, what can you do to encourage them?

4. How familiar are you with the principles of spiritual warfare? How necessary do you see these principles to be at this stage of discipleship?

5. "Bowing the knee" implies both submission and worship. How does this relate to being a "knee-deep Christian"?

6. How can you grow the people you are discipling past knee-deep waters and into a deeper walk with God?

5

waist-deep

What a joy for those whose strength comes from the LORD, who have set their minds on a pilgrimage to Jerusalem. When they walk through the Valley of Weeping, it will become a place of refreshing springs. The autumn rains will clothe it with blessings. They will continue to grow stronger, and each of them will appear before God in Jerusalem.

— PSALM 84:5-7, NLT

Picture two large mountains with a deep valley in between. You are on one side, but you are longing to be on the other. It's almost like picturing yourself where you currently are, and then looking over to where you want to be. In the valley is what I call a "tunnel of chaos." All kinds of past sin not dealt with, wounds from people who sinned against you, conflict you've avoided, shame, and relationship struggles that are unresolved, all of these things reside in the valley beneath the two mountains. You have climbed up one mountain, and now a choice has to be made: either turn back or jump into the valley of the tunnel of chaos in order to get to the other side. This is the precipice where the waist-deep disciple stands.

Who They Are

Let's define those who might be considered waist-deep:

- They know Jesus as Savior and Lord and are beginning to hear the Holy Spirit speak to them. They want to hear from the

91

Lord, and they are looking for what they can do to place themselves in a way to better hear Him and follow His leading. They will be wondering if the voice they heard was Satan, themselves, or the Lord. They are longing to be sheep who know His voice and follow Him [see John 10:3-4], and they are willing to place themselves in the best position to hear from Him.

• They are being confronted with broken places within their hearts and souls that need to be made whole. The Father is surfacing areas of sin, shame, struggle, and conflict in their past that are holding them back from moving forward with Him. He longs to heal them and be with them as they go through the process, and they will have to choose to let Jehovah Rapha heal them so that they can forget what is behind and press on toward what is ahead (see Philippians 3:13).

Where They Are

Waist-deep disciples have complete vulnerability in your relationship. Because good, healthy relationships are important to them, and because you have proved yourself trustworthy, they feel safe enough with you to fully disclose their hearts to you. As they venture out to allow some deep work to take place in their hearts, they will need you to be that safe place where they are fully known and fully loved. This is paramount to their ability to understand the heart of God as they uncover some deep seeds of sin and shame found within them.

One of the most beautiful transitions I have ever experienced when it comes to discipleship was when I began to watch my girls slowly open their hearts to deep places of woundedness and pain. Though it is hard to see them cry, at the same time, I know that freedom is just around the corner for each of them, and that is an incredibly humbling thing to be a part of.

Waist-deep disciples have rekindled eagerness. As they've come to the place of understanding that there will always be more and more to learn and more growing to do in relationship with God and others, you will begin to see a new fire of enthusiasm stirring within them. They will become excited about walking out their new identity and living in authentic relationship with God and others. They will be eager to grow in wholeness and yet they may be apprehensive at the same time. Your love for them and your sharing of your own journey through this process is so valuable and motivating for them to press into their own journeys and find wholeness.

Waist-deep disciples will have a greater awareness. A new set of lenses has now been put on these disciples' eyes. They are now beginning to see life through biblical lenses and they are recognizing spiritual warfare as never before. They are learning to ask, *What does the Bible say about that?* when they are faced with decisions, and they are learning to put on the armor of God to fight the Enemy. As they see his crafty schemes to get them sidetracked in their walk with God, they are learning to overcome him and walk in freedom.

Waist-deep disciples are more assured. Because they have walked alongside you, watching and imitating you, waist-deep disciples are learning to do the things you do, building within themselves a greater confidence in obeying the Word, whether it makes sense or not. They are choosing to live by faith, obeying the Word of God, despite their feelings, because they know God's heart toward them is good. And they are assured that even in their failures, God is there to pick them up and keep moving forward with them.

Waist-deep disciples are becoming learned. The intelligence of waist-deep disciples has turned to wisdom as they are now putting into practice what they have learned and are finding that it works. They are discovering that true wisdom comes when they are confident enough in God and His Word that they act upon it. This newfound wisdom is not something that they share in order that others find them to be smart, but rather they share it in order to tell people that God's way works. They now have personal stories about how they have responded with God's Word and found it to be true.

Because they are now convinced, they are boldly proclaiming what they have learned, especially because they know how much it has changed their lives.

Waist-deep disciples have faith in action. Remember that at the heart of this next generation is a deep desire to not just talk about things, but to back them up with action. They have come to understand the deep love of God, and now, more than ever, they want to *be* the love of God to those around them. They don't want to proclaim His love; they want to practice His love, and now they feel competent and confident enough to do it. The neat thing you will get to witness is that as they begin to share their stories about what God is doing in their lives, they are actually becoming disciplers themselves. While you will be releasing them to do more and more of this on their own, they will still need your encouragement, partnership, availability, and listening ear.

How to Respond to the Waist-Deep Disciple

As disciples begin the journey of living out their faith, while still delving into areas in their lives that are holding them back, their overzealousness must be tempered with your guidance that's training them to keep themselves in a posture to hear from the Lord. They will need to be given the tools to keep themselves hearing from the Father as He lovingly reveals strongholds and opens their eyes to the specific gifts He has placed within them to display His glory. At this point on their discipleship path, they will need to become *equipped*.

Wisdom from Past Generations
Discipline is the refining fire by which talent becomes ability.
— Roy L. Smith, twentieth-century Christian author

Equip

When it comes to this word *equip*, three verses are critical to helping us understand what it looks like:

He handed out gifts above and below, filled heaven with his gifts, filled earth with his gifts. He handed out gifts of apostle, prophet, evangelist, and pastor-teacher to train [equip] Christ's followers in skilled servant work, working within Christ's body, the church, until we're all moving rhythmically and easily with each other, efficient and graceful in response to God's Son, fully mature adults, fully developed within and without, fully alive like Christ. (Ephesians 4:10-13)

There is so much to be discovered in this Scripture that we could delve into it for days! However, Paul was saying that Christians are graced with specific gifts in order to build up the body of Christ, the church, until the fullness of Christ is being manifested in and through every disciple. Everyone has a part to play, but here's the question before us: If the Millennial generation is averse to the church, then how will the fullness of Christ be displayed? This is a big, big deal! Part of your equipping will be to help them see that the purpose for their God-given gifts is to edify the church. And this means that *they are needed* in the church. This fact then invites and commands them to come back to, or join for the first time, a body of believers—and not just attend but edify that body by using their gifts.

The word *train*, or *equip*, in this verse is a translation of the word *katartizo*, which has a twofold meaning: One is "to mend what has been broken; repair; to render fit, sound, and complete." God has some work to do in the hearts of His disciples to mend broken places so they can be completely healed. As you help them sort through their personal "tunnel of chaos," you will be able to speak truth to them and pray for them, offering comfort and support through the Word of God. God will use you in a powerful way to mend some deeply broken places within their souls, as you make yourself available both to Him and to them.

The second part of the definition is "to arrange, prepare and strengthen so that they can be what they were made to be." God wants to mend their hearts so that He can use them mightily, but they will have to align themselves in such a way that they can hear from Him.

Through the process, they will have to know what God says about them. They will need His constant presence and love. Your part in this is to teach the disciple how to discipline herself to live life "tuned in" to the voice of her Savior. There will need to be training on how to keep her heart and ears attentive to His voice. It is only when she arranges her life in a way to hear from the Lord that she will cast off who she is not and embrace becoming all God intends her to be.

Another passage of Scripture, Hebrews 13:20-21, says, "May God, who puts all things together . . . now put you together, [and] provide you with everything you need to please him."

The phrase "provide you with" here is the same word, *katartizo*. God is going to thoroughly mend and prepare His disciples in every way so that they can fulfill the purposes for which they were created, pleasing their Father. And the beauty in this verse is that God will accomplish this because Jesus Christ brought us back into relationship with the Father through His death and resurrection. God didn't just command us to fulfill His desires for us and then leave us to figure it out on our own. He is going to do the work *in us* as we surrender to His loving hands, allowing Him to mold us and make us. What an awesome gift we have inherited through our salvation! We have been given the ability to walk with God and allow Him to re-create us to fulfill the purposes for which He made us.

And finally, God shows us how He will accomplish this in 2 Timothy 3:16-17: "Every part of Scripture is God-breathed and useful one way or another—showing us truth, exposing our rebellion, correcting our mistakes, training us to live God's way. Through the Word we are put together and shaped up ['equipped' (NIV)] for the tasks God has for us."

The word *equipped* here is another word, *exartizo*, and it means "to fully complete; finish; accomplish; to render the days complete." It is vital that the disciple become a lover and a student of the Word of God. It will be the tool God uses most and best to accomplish this work in her life. He wants her to become whole so she can be free to live the abundant life He planned for her, instead of wallowing in her "issues." His Word will teach, reprove, correct, and train her in right living with Him and others. As she stays in His Word, she will find *complete* healing. God will render her days of wallowing in sin and shame of the past complete, done, and finished, so that she can throw off the weight and move forward in freedom with what God has for her. Praise God that this amazing freedom is available to *all* of His disciples! You will be a strategic part in training disciples to discipline their lives to know this about the Word: It will be a lamp to their feet and a light to their path, more to be desired than much fine gold, honey to their lips, and the very Bread of Life that gives them sustenance and strength to live out who God made them to be.

Inspiration from God's Word

Do you see what this means — all these pioneers who blazed the way, all these veterans cheering us on? It means we'd better get on with it. Strip down, start running — and never quit! No extra spiritual fat, no parasitic sins. Keep your eyes on *Jesus*, who both began and finished this race we're in. Study how he did it. Because he never lost sight of where he was headed — that exhilarating finish in and with God — he could put up with anything along the way: Cross, shame, whatever. And now he's *there*, in the place of honor, right alongside God. When you find yourselves flagging in your faith, go over that story again, item by item, that long litany of hostility he plowed through. *That* will shoot adrenaline into your souls!

— Hebrews 12:1-3

You may find that part of your help in equipping them will be to also help them discover their spiritual gifts, talents, and abilities that God created in them. They may need you to observe and tell them what you see that comes naturally to them, what passions they have, and how you could see them using those gifts to edify the body of

Christ. Your speaking these blessings into their lives may be the first time they have ever seen their worth in God's "big story" of their life.

As they begin to delve into their brokenness, you will be able to help them make the connection that their greatest *misery* could become their greatest *ministry* within the church. You could help them turn their pain into a passion to help others, so that they will feel that what they went through was not in vain, but rather a season of preparation for what God has for them to do in the future. You may even search out places where they could slowly begin to serve in ministry based on the gifts and passions they have. You may be the very one who can place them in opportunities for them to thrive in their gifts.

You will be equipping them by offering them the following:

Less direction. Like a mother bird, kicking her babies out of the nest to let them fly, you will now be letting this disciple try out her new set of wings. You will offer less hand-holding, but you will still offer lots of talking about what God would have her do, and you will be consistently available for her whenever she needs you. You will provide a security to fall back on as she is trying to walk on her own. Pointing her to Immanuel, the with-us, always-present God, is essential to her growth.

I can remember trying to teach my children how to ride a bike. I would hold on to the back of my child's bicycle, steadying each of them as they learned balance, steering, and how to pedal down the road. As they learn to ride the paths of walking with God and living in light of His presence, disciples will need your steady hand of love, grace, and guidance to point them to the One who gives them the power to be all that they were created to be.

Growing affirmation. As disciples are learning about relating to God and others, warring to overcome the Enemy, grasping their newfound identity, and seeking to become whole, they will need you there with them, affirming their righteous choices. You will be like a cheerleader for them as you inspire and urge them on in living out all that they have learned. Showing your approval and agreeing with their good choices gives them the security and strength needed for them to keep going.

Consistent communication. Disciples will be looking to you to give them all that they need to move from wisdom to action. Though they are eager to get busy living out what they are learning, they also need to make sure that they have aligned themselves with certain disciplines in their lives in order to maintain their walk with God while they serve. If these tools are not provided, busyness will overtake their lives and hearing from God will be overcome by the roaring demands of life. If these distractions are not kept in check, their Christianity will be minimized to a lot of action apart from the Shepherd's guidance, support, friendship, and power. And most of us can attest from experience that it is not a good thing to exchange spiritual intimacy for religious activity.

Intentional availability. A great support for a disciple who is stepping out on her own is the knowledge that someone is right there with her in both her successes and her failures. If she gets caught in a situation in which she is questioning a decision or realizing that she is responding in the same old past, negative ways in specific situations, she will need to know that you are accessible to help, pray, exhort, and refocus her in the right direction.

There may come a time when God surfaces a very deep wound of sexual sin, addiction, or even abuse. You, as the discipler, may feel that this is more than you can handle or that she needs some in-depth Christian counseling to help her find her healing. It is crucial that you do not leave her, but rather ask her to prayerfully consider going to counseling, in addition to continuing your relationship. You may even offer to go with her and be there with her every step of the way. There is nothing worse than for disciples to reveal a naked, vulnerable place within themselves and then have you respond with shock and send them off to someone else who will get them "fixed." It makes them feel as if they have the plague, and it usually results in their quickly covering back up—and resolving to never do that again.

If you find yourself in a place where a disciple needs counseling, please contact us at LivingDeeperMinistries.com, and we will connect you with a Christian counselor in your area who can both help your disciple and also help you know how to best come alongside and support her through the process.

When my son Cole was learning to sleep by himself in his bed, I had to first lie in bed with him until he fell asleep. Then I would sit by his bed. Then I would sit outside his room. For the first several nights, I would hear him call out, "Are you there, Mom?" I would assure him of my presence, and he then felt secure enough to overcome his fear and fall asleep. Those whom you disciple will need the same thing. They will need the confident assurance of your presence with them.

The waist is the middle and narrowest part of our bodies. Sometimes referred to in Scripture with the word *loins*, the waist was where a belt was placed to hold a person's garments up and together, so he could be free from hindrances and not stumble as he moved from place to place. The loins were also to be well-protected, because that was the place where generational seed resided.

As a disciple walks into waist-deep waters with Jesus Christ, she has made the choice to jump into the middle of the tunnel of chaos and fight for her freedom. And while working through the past that has entangled her, a narrowing takes place. Just as the waist narrows, there is a narrowing of focus in the spirit. No longer do other things capture the attention that they had received in the past. The disciple's eyes are narrowed to God's path for her life, and she has her face "set like flint" as she presses in and presses onward toward freedom from the entanglements of her past.

Not only does a narrowing take place, but a girding also occurs. First Peter 1:13 says to "gird up the loins of your mind" (KJV). Peter was speaking in terms the people could understand. In biblical times, clothing was such that in order for them to move about freely without their garments getting in the way, they would have to gather up the excess fabric and tuck it into their belts. Through the process of being delivered from the past, it is important that disciples gather up God's Word, His truth, to hold their minds together when the Enemy seeks to drag them back to their past with his lies. As a discipler, you must help them discipline themselves to cling to the truth of who God says they are in His Word.

Paul even said it like this in Ephesians 6:14, as he described the first piece of armor: "Stand therefore, having your loins *girt about* with truth" (KJV, emphasis added). Paul was saying that the first piece of armor with which we take our stand against the Enemy, and wade through the tunnel of chaos, is the belt of truth. Belts hold things together.

The word *girded* here means "to fasten as with a belt, to equip one's self with the knowledge of truth." Disciples must learn to cling to the truth when the Enemy comes against them with lies. They must have God's Word tightly girded around their minds, reminding them of who they are and who God created them to be. Knowing the truth is what will equip them to stand firm when the Enemy tries to trip them up.

In the book of Jeremiah, God commanded the prophet to take a linen waistband and put it around his waist. At that time, linen was a mark of the priesthood, those who were privileged enough to enter God's presence. This waistband was an undergarment that directly touched the skin where the reproductive parts were. This was a symbol of intimacy and fruitful seed. In Jeremiah 13:11, God says, "As a loincloth [waistband] clings to a man's waist, so I created Judah and Israel to cling to me, says the LORD. They were to be my people, my pride, my glory—an honor to my name. But they would not listen to me" (NLT).

What God is saying through these three Scriptures is this: Just like a linen belt, He wants an intimate relationship with us, one in which we can live freely and continually in His presence. He wants our minds fastened to, clinging to, and held together with His truth, so that when we face the Enemy's lies, His truth is tightly bound to the central core of who we are. We have it so well tucked within our souls that the Enemy's lies do not trip us up as we seek to run this race with our Father. This truth is a sacred seed that He places within us because His desire has always been for us to reproduce. As He plants the seeds of truth in our lives, we give birth to that truth to those around us. God created us to "be fruitful, and multiply" (Genesis 1:28, KJV), and He will implant Himself and His truth in the waist-deep disciple, preparing her to reproduce other Christ-followers as she holds forth the Word of truth, the Word of life.

Wisdom from Past Generations

When all things are right between you and the Lord, you can be a spiritual parent.

— DAWSON TROTMAN, EVANGELIST AND FOUNDER OF THE NAVIGATORS

What a joy it will be for you to watch the fruit of your sowing into the heart of another bloom forth. You have sown much truth into the soil of her heart, producing a beautiful disciple of Jesus Christ. What a delight it will be when you begin to see her giving birth and discipling another. This has always been God's heart. He chose to live in this world and accomplish His purposes through us as we reproduce disciples. How humbling that we get to be a part of it.

Deeper Reflections

1. Do you know anyone who is "waist-deep" in the discipleship process? What is her story? What practical things can you do to reach her?

2. Where are you when it comes to the characteristics of a "waist-deep Christian"? Which of the defining characteristics — complete vulnerability, rekindled

eagerness, greater awareness, more assurance, greater wisdom, or faith put into action — best describes you? What ultimately helps you move on past this stage?

3. One of the developments in this stage is frequently the revealing of places of deep woundedness and pain in the heart of the one you are discipling. What can you do to prepare for such revelations should they come? How do you feel about this aspect of the discipleship process? How can you help your disciple transform her greatest *misery* into her greatest *ministry*?

4. Which of the strategies for equipping (providing less direction, growing affirmation, consistent communication, and constant availability) do you find the easiest? The most challenging? Why?

5. How can you grow the person you are discipling past waist-deep waters and into a deeper walk with God?

6

over the head

We teach what we know; we reproduce what we are.

— ROBERT SCHMIDGALL

I'll never forget learning how to jump off the diving board. It was the strangest emotional mixture of both fear and excitement at the same time. I stood on the edge of that board for what seemed like hours, others even pushing me aside to jump off ahead of me. I saw them jump, and I wanted so badly to jump in and enjoy the swim just like them, but the unknown kept me on the side. Finally, whether in a weak moment of abandon, or a strong moment of bravery, in one split second, I jumped! I can remember coming up out of the water with this exhilaration and resolve to do that again, and again, and again. Once I jumped, there was no turning back. I was in on the diving scene and loving every minute of it. And not only was I in the cycle from the board to the stairs and back in line for the next jump, I had invited everybody else at the pool to join me. I couldn't keep this newfound experience a secret.

These are exactly the feelings of disciples who are over the head in love with Jesus Christ. Whereas they may have been scared and skeptical at first, once they jump in, get acclimated to the waters, and begin to move with them, the joy of living deeper with the Father has permeated them to their core. It's where they want to be, it's where they want to stay, and it's where they want everyone else to be as well!

Who They Are

Let's define those who might be considered over the head:

- They have developed a growing intimacy with the Father, hearing His voice, following His voice, and experiencing the abundant life that walking with Him brings.
- They recognize that though they have learned much, relationship and spiritual growth is always a process as the various seasons of life emerge.
- They have developed a growing desire to not only be a disciple but to become a discipler as they have watched you model how to spiritually parent another.

Wisdom from Past Generations

Faith is a living, bold trust in God's grace, so certain of God's favor that it would risk death a thousand times trusting in it. Such confidence and knowledge of God's grace makes you happy, joyful, and bold in your relationship to God and all creatures. The Holy Spirit makes this happen through faith. Because of it, you freely, willingly, and joyfully do good to everyone, serve everyone, suffer all kinds of things, and love and praise the God who has shown you such grace.

— MARTIN LUTHER, SIXTEENTH-CENTURY PROTESTANT REFORMER

Where They Are

Over-the-head disciples have a refashioned eagerness. Whereas in ankle-deep waters of discipleship they had been cautiously eager, now they are enthusiastically eager to continue to grow, no longer afraid of admitting their lack of understanding. They are humbly seeking and are meek and teachable.

Thoughts from Present-Day Leaders

What makes authentic disciples is not visions, ecstasies, biblical mastery of chapter and verse, or spectacular success in the ministry, but a capacity for faithfulness. Buffeted by the fickle winds of failure, battered by their own unruly emotions, and bruised by rejection and ridicule, authentic disciples may have stumbled and frequently fallen, endured lapses and relapses, gotten handcuffed to the fleshpots and wandered into a far country. Yet, they kept coming back to Jesus.

— BRENNAN MANNING, IN THE RAGAMUFFIN GOSPEL

Over-the-head disciples have a regenerated assurance. Whereas in ankle-deep waters they were self-assured, they have now developed the confidence in God to complete everything for which He has created them and to which He has called them to be. They can look back and see the doors they have been through and how God has brought them so far. They can see the doors around them, revealing opportunities where they can now serve. They can also see the doors that still lie ahead and all the exciting possibilities in store as they continue to walk and trust in the Father. All three of these things have instilled in them a confidence in the faithfulness of God.

Inspiration from God's Word

Consider it a sheer gift, friends, when tests and challenges come at you from all sides. You know that under pressure, your faith-life is forced into the open and shows its true colors. So don't try to get out of anything prematurely. Let it do its work so you become mature and well-developed, not deficient in any way.

— JAMES 1:2-4

Over-the-head disciples have a re-created awareness. Where once life's circumstances were nothing more than a bunch of unrelated inconveniences to be quickly fixed, the over-the-head disciple actually welcomes and offers thanksgiving for trials and struggles because she anticipates the growth and deepening intimacy that will result. She no longer lets her circumstances define her, but rather she is letting her circumstances help her find God in a deeper way.

Over-the-head disciples have a reshaped learning. Instead of simply being intellectually sound, they have grown to become wise. Wisdom develops when the intelligence we have gained is tested by practice and found to work. As disciples grow, they have gone from saying, "I know everything," to "I know nothing," to "I know some," to "I know certainly." This growing wisdom is what will motivate them to share their faith with others as they have seen the positive results from living out God's truths in their lives.

How to Respond

Jesus had readied His disciples to go and do just as He had done. He had taught them principles of godly living and had not only lived them out before them, but had given them opportunities to live them out, as well. Jesus had made an abundance of investments, and now it was time for Him to pass the proverbial torch to the disciples: "When the Holy Spirit comes on you, you will be able [have power] to be my witnesses in Jerusalem, all over Judea and Samaria, even to the ends of the world" (Acts 1:8). You, too, have been investing in disciples of Christ. Now it is time for you to *empower* them to go and make disciples.

Thoughts from Present-Day Leaders

The closest contemporary word to "disciple" is probably "apprentice." A disciple is more than a student who learns lessons by means of lectures or books. He is one who learns by living and working with his teacher in a daily "hands on" experience.

— Warren Wiersbe, pastor and Christian author

Empower

The word *empower* in the Old Testament is the Hebrew word *shalat*, and it means "to give power to; to master, lord over, or give domination to; to exercise power over." It is the same word rendered in several Old Testament Scriptures as "dominion." Psalm 119:133 says, "Order my steps in thy word: and let not any iniquity have dominion over me" (KJV). What does God want us as disciples to understand? God wants His Word to master and guide our lives, not troubles, sorrow, or sin. He no longer wants us to exert ourselves on things that really don't matter. He no longer wants us to be held back, exhausting ourselves, as we wallow in our past. He wants us to live through the promised Holy Spirit as the power source that dominates our lives, so we can spend ourselves on advancing His kingdom by making more disciples on the earth.

In Acts 1:8 above, the New Testament word *power* is the Greek word *dynamis*, and it means "power within which is exerted out." Our word *dynamite* comes from this word. The dynamite I have experienced is loud and effective! This power is described as moral power, miraculous power, and molding power. An over-the-head disciple must understand that the Holy Spirit has been implanted within her to be the dominating force, no longer being dominated by sin and self.

How freeing to know that instead of exerting all kinds of energy to feel whole, successful, and free, a disciple can simply surrender complete control and allow the power of the Holy Spirit to take over. His power enables the disciple to live a moral life, to be a part of miraculous experiences of healing and hope, and to influence others by helping them yield to God's molding of Himself in them.

What a delight to follow in the footsteps of Jesus, and empower disciples to know, grow, go, and show, evidence that they are passionate followers of Jesus Christ.

Know. Before now, you have taken disciples by the hand and helped them grasp the hand of God. You have guided them along the path of discipleship, and as they have grown into maturity, it is time for them to be completely guided by the Spirit. John 10:4-5 says, "He calls his own sheep by name and leads them out. When he gets them all out, he leads them and they follow because they are familiar with his voice. They won't follow a stranger's voice but will scatter because they aren't used to the sound of it." They have grown to know and follow the Good Shepherd's voice. Jesus said, "If you stick with this, living out what I tell you, you are my disciples for sure. Then you will experience for yourselves the truth, and the truth will free you" (John 8:31-32). They have begun to know Jesus intimately and the truths found in His Word, and are convinced that obedience to His truth is where freedom is truly found. Now it is time for you to give them less direction so that they can receive most of their guidance and direction from the Holy Spirit. Empower them to hear God's voice and obey Him no matter how they feel, because they trust wholeheartedly in the Shepherd of their hearts.

Grow. This journey of discipleship must be embraced as a process of the disciples' learning to believe in themselves as God overcomes their past, preprogrammed beliefs about themselves that have given them a limited view of what God has created in them. Their belief system has held them captive and restricted who they are and what they are capable of achieving. But as they grow with Him, God reveals that He has given them the ability to be a phenomenal person who is empowered to accomplish incredible things for His glory. The challenge is finding what frees them to come alive, fires them up, and feeds their souls. As you help disciples grow in this, they will abandon themselves to reach their God-given goals wholeheartedly. Your part, then, is to surround them with the confidence that you believe in them. You believe in the God who lives in them. This is a vital ingredient for them to reach their full potential. If you can help develop in them an unshakable belief in who Christ is in them and the role that they are destined to play, then there are no limits or boundaries to restrict the powerful possibilities that lie in store for them.

Go. In Mark 16:15, Jesus said to the disciples, "Go into the world. Go everywhere and announce the Message of God's good news to one and all." That word *go* is *poreuo,* and it means "to pursue the journey upon which one has entered." Now is the time for you to empower the disciple whom God has given you to go and do what He has placed in her heart to do.

Thoughts from Present-Day Leaders

Jesus' plan called for action, and how He expressed it predicted its success. He didn't say "you might be My witnesses," or "you could be My witnesses," or even "you should be My witnesses." He said, "You will be My witnesses."

— CHARLES R. SWINDOLL, PASTOR AND CHRISTIAN AUTHOR

In Luke 9, tons of people had spent the day listening to Jesus, and they were all hungry. The disciples came to Jesus to get His help. Jesus answered, "You feed them!" He had already empowered them to do miraculous things through the power of the Spirit. Jesus was empowering them to do what He placed inside of them to do for His glory.

You now get the chance to do the same. Customize opportunities for your disciple that best fit the passions, talents, and abilities that you have observed coming forth from her. Join her and watch her come alive as she finds her "sweet spot" in fulfilling the purposes for which she was created. It will be the most rewarding feeling you've ever experienced as you see the eternal fruit borne from your impact.

With my young women, I planned a Sunday afternoon and evening to go and serve at a homeless shelter. I put a girl in my group, who is a budding leader, in charge of overseeing what we do. I put a worship leader in our group in charge of planning a worship service for the evening. I am putting a very crafty girl in charge of the crafts we will do, and the other two girls will be helping in preparing the meal we will serve.

Show. Often when Jesus healed someone, He would instruct him to go and show himself to others who didn't believe. Also, when Jesus raised His friend Lazarus from the dead, Lazarus came forth bound in burial linens. Jesus said, "Unwrap him and let him loose" (John 11:44). You see, as you have discipled others, you have helped them get out of bondage to all kinds of sin, shame, and pain. Now they get the chance to go and do the same for others. One of the final thrills of a discipler is to empower disciples to go and show others how to believe in the Lord Jesus Christ and become disciples, as well. You send them out to "unwrap others and let them go." To say to disciples, "I have watched God do incredible things in and through your life, and now I believe you are ready to disciple another," inspires them and gives them a boost of confidence that says you believe that they have what it takes. This consistent spiritual communication is commissioning them to go and make disciples just as you have done with them. There's nothing better than their knowing that not only do you believe in them enough to entrust them with this mission, but that God believes in them enough to entrust them with this mission, as well. God chose them to show others how to walk with Him, so empower them to show off.

Wisdom from Past Generations
There are no crown wearers in heaven who were not cross bearers here below.
— CHARLES H. SPURGEON, NINETEENTH-CENTURY BAPTIST PREACHER

Every once in a while, my husband longs for a yummy, juicy steak. He will tenderize that meat and then marinate it for several hours until the meat is completely permeated with the special sauce. There is not one part of that meat that has not been affected by the tangy and sweet sauce. Being led by God into the deepest of waters, until it is over our heads, is much like my husband's steak. It takes place when we are completely affected and overtaken by the Holy Spirit, when we are no longer seen because who we are has been overtaken by all of who God is within us. Paul said it like this:

> Indeed, I have been crucified with Christ. My ego is no longer central. It is no longer important that I appear righteous before you or have your good opinion, and I am no longer driven to impress God. Christ lives in me. The life you see me living is not "mine," but it is lived by faith in the Son of God, who loved me and gave himself for me. I am not going to go back on that. (Galatians 2:20-21)

When Scripture uses the words "over the head" in the Ezekiel 47 description of the pathway of discipleship, it is synonymous with the words "pass over" and "cross over." All three phrases are used to describe any kind of transition being made, as well as "to cover."

If you remember a time of jumping into the deep end of a swimming pool, you also remember that a definite transition was made as you went from thoroughly dry to completely soaked in a moment. Once you took the plunge, there was not a single place on your body not affected by the water. You were covered with water from head to toe.

God's desire for every one of His disciples is to be completely soaked, overtaken, saturated, and covered by Himself. He wants us to walk with Him in such intimate fellowship that all of who He is becomes all of who we are. He wants to be included in every part of your day, even the menial tasks. He wants to be included as you do everything with Him and for Him. He wants you to have such an awareness of His overtaking, constant presence that you experience an abundant life, filled with joy and victory in spite of life's circumstances, because He is with you. And one of the benefits is that others in His creation may see an accurate representation of what He looks like and want to walk with Him too. He wants to completely transform us back to the way He originally designed us to be at Creation:

holy and whole, walking with Him throughout the day, enjoying His presence.

When the children of Israel were slaves in Egypt, God was with them when He sent the angel of death to the Egyptians but "passed over" His chosen people. Once they were let go, God parted the waters so they could "cross over" and head toward the Promised Land. The children of Israel made some transitions from death to life, from captivity to freedom, from pain to promise. As a disciple, you have done the same thing. Because you have been covered by the precious blood of Jesus Christ, you have moved from independence to total dependence, from selfishness to selflessness, from lies to truth, from brokenness to wholeness, from old to new, from control to surrender, and from living by your flesh to living by the Spirit. You are headed for the Promised Land, and God wants you to take some folks with you!

I grew up in south Georgia, where pine trees are in abundance. My dad would call me out on a fall Saturday morning to help him rake all of the needles that had peppered our yard. Because my hands would get blisters on them, my dad always had me wear a pair of good ol' working gloves. He even set them out for me! Once I had those coverings on my hands, I was able to do the work while being protected from injury. One morning, as I sat there eating my bowl of cereal and staring at those gloves I was about to don, I recognized that the gloves were useless until I put my hands in them. But once my hands did go in those gloves, I could do all kinds of things without fear of hurting my hands.

As disciples of Jesus Christ, we are nothing but an empty glove until we allow Christ to fill us. Jesus said in John 15 that apart from Him, we can do nothing, so what we do apart from His hand within us really is for nothing. But once we allow His hand to fill our life's glove, He empowers us to do things to advance His kingdom that we could have never imagined in our wildest dreams! He guides, leads, and controls our every move, protecting us from getting spiritual blisters and suffering from burnout as we live in the calling He planned for us. Jesus said it like this: "See what I've given you? Safe passage as you walk on snakes and scorpions, and protection from every assault of the Enemy. No one can put a hand on you" (Luke 10:19). From the moment of salvation (know), God has been preparing us (grow) and has empowered us to advance the gospel (go), make disciples (show), and step on the Enemy when he tries to get in the way. It's an abundant, fulfilling life that He generously offers, but sadly so few of us find this life this side of eternity.

Many people are in over their heads with stress, financial debt, busyness, schedules, demands, relational struggles, and more. They find no joy, peace, rest, or meaning for their lives. They merely exist, chasing a pursuit that they think may give them enough security to get some relief, yet all the while, they are running and getting nowhere as the stressors of life continue to mount. They are in over their heads and miserable.

But not you. You have chosen to make another disciple, to pour into her and let God lead you both out into deeper waters of living with Him. You have jumped in over your head, and you are now soaked to the bone with the presence and power of the Holy Spirit within. You are living out the plans and purposes for which you were created, and you are empowering another to go and do the same. This is the most fulfilling mission of which to be a part. And those who choose this path are truly in over their heads and loving it!

Deeper Reflections

1. Do you remember the first time you jumped off a diving board? What was it like to feel "in over your head"? Exhilarating? Terrifying? A little of both? Tell the story.
2. Do you know anyone who is in "over her head" in the discipleship process? Are you there yourself? What is it like?

3. Which of the defining characteristics of those in "over the head" in discipleship—refashioned eagerness, regenerated assurance, re-created awareness, or reshaped learning—excites you the most about this stage? Which excites you the least? Why do you suppose that is?

4. Explain in your own words what the "power of the Holy Spirit" means to you. How has it helped you in your own Christian walk? How can it (or has it) helped your disciple to do the same?

5. How has your disciple exhibited "power" in each of these four areas? In which area is she the strongest? The weakest? How can you help serve to shore up her weak areas?

   • Know:
   • Grow:
   • Go:
   • Show:

6. How do you feel about potentially releasing your disciple out into the world for her to become a discipler herself? Any mixed emotions? How well-prepared do you believe she is? What more needs to be accomplished in her life before you can (or should) release her and commission her to go and make disciples herself?

7

the pool is open

As a parent, it seems you always try to be prepared for whatever might arise in your family. Since you just never know what you might need and when you might need it, you think of every possible scenario and prepare accordingly. Going to the pool is no different. You pack drinks, snacks, towels, tanning lotion, sunscreen, toys, floats, iPods, a book to read, and so on, in the event that any of these things will be needed. Better to be prepared than destitute!

My prayer has certainly been that this book has awakened you to the desperate need for discipleship for the future of the church and this amazing and dynamic generation coming behind us. My hope is that you will take up the mantle and join me and a vast army of women to band together and begin a discipling revolution in our nation. My desire is to create in you a sense of urgency to help the Millennials start living deeper in the waters of relationship with Jesus Christ, before we lose them to our downward-spiraling culture.

I have tried my best to articulate what you might expect as you journey with this wonderful next generation: how they think, what influences them, what is important to them, and how best to come alongside them in the discipling process. Not only have I sought to enlighten you regarding the souls of Millennials, I have also tried to encourage you in how to best lead them through each successive stage of their journey with Jesus. I also hope that as you have learned about being a discipler, you have also been discipled as you have journeyed through these pages. God is so good that in the process of discipling another, we are surprised to find that we are being discipled at the very same time.

As I reviewed my own discipleship process, God revealed to me seven areas that are needed to take disciples from ankle-deep to over their heads through the discipling process. So, if you've wondered what to study and what it means practically, to be *living deeper*, I've created a guide for each topic. I'll tell you more about those later, but first I simply want to share the truths He put on my heart.

Relationships

Due to wounded pasts and misguided influences, the beauty and purposes of relationships have been lost. Disciples need guidance in establishing a healthy relationship with God and with others. We also need to know how to progress with God and His purposes at the center of friendships. Since God is a relational God and He created us in His image, then we are relational people. And yet, it seems that relationships are just so hard! I have even heard it said that life would be so much better if it weren't for people.

God intended for relationships to be fulfilling, encouraging, challenging, inspiring, and full of life, and yet we often don't feel that way about them at all. Disciples need to be taken deeper into understanding God's purposes for relationships, and encouraged to live out those purposes with those around them. As they connect more in their relationship with God, they will begin to connect better with others and grow into a mature community of disciples and disciple makers. Before someone is willing to hear what we believe about a loving God, she should experience being loved by His people. Strong, healthy relationships are the foundation of a discipleship revolution.

Wisdom from Past Generations
No road is too long in the company of a friend.

— Japanese proverb

God
Any good story has some sort of love story intertwined within its pages. We long for these stories where love overcomes, conquers, and wins over the evil that threatens to ruin this beautiful romance. And yet, when we look at God and our relationship with Him, we can easily lose sight of the love story — a love story in which we are the object of His love and affection. The Bible, like a love story unfolding before our eyes, reveals that though God is described in many ways and as many things, He is ultimately and completely love in its truest form. Disciples must be enlightened to the Lover of their souls, who has been pursuing them since before they took their first breath and longs to be their Eternal Beloved. Living in this covenant of love enables disciples to discover how God sees them and how they are to live in light of this life-altering reality. This love takes us deeper, returning us to living with God in newfound joy, adventure, intrigue, and wonder. When we begin to view God as *love*, we begin to truly live as part of His story.

Wisdom from Past Generations
Disregard the study of God, and you sentence yourself to stumble and blunder through life blindfolded, as it were, with no sense of direction and no understanding of what surrounds you.

— Charles H. Spurgeon, nineteenth-century Baptist preacher

Spiritual Warfare

In a world where Satan has been minimized to a little man in a red suit, with pointed tail and pitchfork in tow, it is vital for disciples to understand that he is their enemy and that he is out to destroy them. He is the great antagonist in the gospel's true love story. Disciples must be made aware of the Enemy's schemes to render them ineffective. They must be empowered to cut through the fog of life's circumstances and understand that a full-on assault of the Enemy aims to destroy the abundant life experienced in relationship with God and His people. We must encourage and equip a disciple to be victorious as she learns how to combat the Enemy and walk in truth. This is a vital part of the Christian's life that is many times overlooked or ignored. It is time to teach Christ's beloved how to fight and overcome an already-defeated foe. This fight requires balance, never allowing spiritual warfare to consume our attention. Become aware and become a warrior, but keep your eyes on Jesus. God can even turn what Satan intends to harm us into something to strengthen you. You can actually find new life as you fight!

Wisdom from Past Generations

I often laugh at Satan, and there is nothing that makes him so angry as when I attack him to his face, and tell him that through God I am more than a match for him.

— MARTIN LUTHER, SIXTEENTH-CENTURY PROTESTANT REFORMER

Identity

Many disciples have been inundated with conflicting messages about who they are and who they were created to be. Where gender lines are blurred and *womanhood* is a confusing label, disciples need to know how uniquely God created them and the feminine characteristics that make them the crown of His creation. To not know who they are is to wander aimlessly through life, love, and spiritual battlefields. We must encourage disciples to rediscover who they are and engage Jesus in a lifelong process of becoming more like Him. Women in your life need help diving into the deeper waters of understanding life in the image of a loving God and living out who He made them to be. When they understand their unique role in God's story, their desires and God's plan collide for a truly epic life!

Thoughts from Present-Day Leaders

The desperate need today is not for a greater number of intelligent people, or gifted people, but for deep people.

— Richard Foster, Christian author

Spiritual Disciplines

A disciple is to be holy, and yet that seems like a tall order, maybe even impossible in today's world. It's one thing to recognize the big picture and major obstacles in our spiritual lives, but it's another to know how to live day to day in the little things that reveal and deepen our relationship with God. Simple actions and attitudes have a tremendous impact on our experiences. Spiritual disciplines are basic habits of a healthy communication, much like any other relationship. It is imperative that a disciple learn to posture herself to focus on the presence of God and to hear His voice so that she can follow His movement and model His ways on earth. Regularly exercising our ability to interact with God profoundly strengthens our character as we develop into His likeness. God wants to take us deeper than a surface-level knowledge, to a reality filled with life-changing experiences in His presence. As disciple makers, we must equip other disciples with the habits and disciplines needed for spiritual health, growth, and depth.

Wholeness

Disciples need to be nurtured. A disciple may have seeds of truth scattered in her heart, but if wounds, shame, past sin, and lies have not been weeded out, it will be as though a layer of concrete covers the soil of her soul. Too many young women are missing out on the abundant life Jesus offers because of the wounds of the past. God offers healing. He wants us to move forward in our future with Him, but until we work through some broken places in our past, we still allow Satan's hook to be in us and hold us captive in the darkness. Once transformation takes place through the light of God's Word and His people, women can really start living free from the overwhelming weight of their pasts. This will equip disciples to go forward with Him in freedom, turning their pain into passion and their greatest misery into their greatest ministry.

Thoughts from Present-Day Leaders

We don't serve God to gain His acceptance; we are accepted so we serve God. We don't follow Him in order to be loved; we are loved, so we follow Him.

— NEIL ANDERSON, CHRISTIAN AUTHOR

Process

Life is always fluid; it changes. And with each change comes more opportunity for growth. Growing never stops until we are perfect and entire, lacking nothing in eternity. It is paramount for disciples and disciple makers to keep in mind that discipleship is a process. No one ever arrives; all are just seeking and striving to be like Jesus. It is the only way we will be happy, fulfilled, and free, living the way God originally created us to be! God never intended for our existence to be lifeless. He wants us to be disciples who will join Him in the process of becoming like Him while going and making more disciples to lock arms with and partner in the journey. Life was meant to be an exciting adventure as God is at work all around us, in us, and through us. Empower women to be both disciples and disciple makers, increasing their influence among family, friends, church, and community. As they join God's revolutionary mission in the process of discipleship, they can grow deeper with Christ and take others with them. After all, *Living Deeper* is all about women helping women walk with God!

Thoughts from Present-Day Leaders

Biblically, waiting is not just something we have to do until we get what we want. Waiting is part of the process of becoming what God wants us to be.

— JOHN ORTBERG, PASTOR AND AUTHOR

I believe with all of my heart that we can change a generation, a culture, and the world when we embrace these seven truths in the depths of our hearts and reproduce them in the lives of others. Once we understand and experience the power of walking with God and the promises of His Word, the next natural step in depth and maturity is to share His abundant life with others. Someone has poured spiritual life into you. Others desperately need spiritual life poured into them. The women you disciple relationally will then pour out the same spiritual waters into the lives of others around them. Healthy disciples naturally become disciple makers. The abundant life overflows from one person to the next!

While the seven areas of discipleship identified above progress in a very intentional order that tracks along with each level of depth — ankle, knee, waist, and over the head — you, as the discipler, will need to ask the Holy Spirit to give you discernment to know when and what the one you are discipling needs. Listen to the Spirit and walk closely with Him, asking Him to show you where you should start. Then, let His Spirit guide you from one topic to the next as He reveals the way. Like a ship, hoist up the sail and let the Spirit direct you through the guides to create a custom fit for each disciple based on where she is in her journey.

If you'd like to go deeper into each of these areas of discipleship, continuing on this revolutionary journey with me, I've written the LIVING DEEPER series with seven experiential guides, uniquely created to help your young women experience God and His truth as they put it into practice. When a disciple is challenged to experience something that she has to go through or live through, she develops a first-hand knowledge. That firsthand knowledge becomes permanent to her because she personally experienced it and knows it works. This is what has been missing in so many educational models: *obedience through application*. Discipleship requires practice; it's an action. I believe in providing various opportunities for a disciple to connect with God in relevant, relational, and applicable ways specifically designed to carry the truths of the Bible into the depths of a person's soul. This type of discipleship will be different from the typical Bible study you may have used in the past or models of multiplication relying purely on theological instruction. Millennials are different from us, and thus they need to be discipled in a way that may seem "out of the box" for us, but refreshing and inviting to them.

I invite you to take what you've read to the next level. I believe that God has offered us a very specific pathway to travel; not just going deeper in knowledge of Him, but truly *living out* the deeper things of Him in our life choices. God doesn't just want us to exist; He wants us to experience an abundant life that is happy, fulfilling, and free. To learn to walk with God, living out His truths and allowing Him to direct our path in the way that He desires, is to open a doorway for us to experience Him more authentically and abundantly. Living deeper with God is the only pathway to abundance and to fulfilling the purposes for which we were created.

Inspiration from God's Word

Everyone who hears these words of mine and puts them into practice is like a wise man who built his house on the rock. The rain came down, the streams rose, and the winds blew and beat against that house; yet it did not fall, because it had its foundation on the rock.
— MATTHEW 7:24-25, NIV

You can use these seven areas of study in either one-on-one discipleship or small-group discipleship. You may choose for these to be more organized and structured in their setting, or you may see these as more laid-back times that are organic: simple, natural, healthful in nature. Time spent with your girls will also simply be activities that you are already doing; they are just invited to join you. Take those you are discipling with you to the grocery store, the mall, and other activities. Simply model the life of a disciple before them. This requires your giving them access to your life, making yourself available. Also, carve out time for lunch or dinner, especially if they are struggling; drop what you are doing and go to them with encouragement. Jesus went about living an example before His disciples in everyday circumstances. Discipleship didn't stop and start; it was a lifestyle for Jesus, and it needs to be the same for us.

The fact that discipleship is an ongoing lifestyle and process does not mean it is routine and predictable—following God is anything but predictable. In Isaiah 55:8 God says, "I don't think the way you think. The way you work isn't the way I work." Jesus healed the blind in several different ways, and He taught His original twelve disciples in different ways. God will use all different kinds of objects in nature, stories, riddles, songs, and activities to help His disciples get to know Him better.

Remember, these topics and the resources developed with these things in mind are to serve as tools and guideposts, not a process that is so structured and rigid that the disciple feels as if she is riding on a production conveyor belt. Pull out what you need, when you need it. Some areas you may move through rather quickly, while others may require a period of time until the disciple has really found freedom or growth in that area. As you let the Holy Spirit guide you, you will be communicating to the one you disciple that she is deeply loved and cared for. She will understand that you just want to come alongside her and walk with her wherever she needs to go for however long she needs to be there.

One of the best ways, I've found, for spiritual truths to find their way from my head into my heart is to reinforce those promises and words of God in music. Worship music connects on an emotional level, keeping the truth fresh and meaningful in the depths of my soul. This is one of the most powerful ways to help people engage God. Worship through music has a way of soothing our souls and ushering the presence of God into our consciousness, so that He can speak to us and change us. Because of this, I'd like to offer you a gift for your journey as a disciple maker. We have developed a compilation of praise and worship music to accompany the biblical truths of each experiential guide. You and the one you disciple will be reading, studying, meditating, and even singing the truths of God's Word, allowing it to permeate your souls in many different ways. One of the greatest things you can do for a disciple is to help her discover the powerful impact worship music has on her spiritual well-being and growth. Find out more about these musical compilations at LivingDeeperMinistries.com.

Finally, I want to come alongside you and your church as you become a discipler! There's nothing quite like hands-on experience as you step into this new adventure. One of my greatest passions is gathering face-to-face with women to see the fires of a discipleship revolution spread! Not only do we get to dive deeper into practical ways to best reach and disciple the next generation, but we get connected relationally for support, prayer, encouragement, and assistance with anything you need. To find out how you can be a part of such a conference, visit us at LivingDeeperMinistries.com.

To write a book that awakens you to the need to disciple and tells you how to disciple but gives you no practical tools with which to disciple the next generation is lacking a huge piece of the pie. I feel that with the leadership of the Holy Spirit, along with these guides and the variety of experiential and training resources available online and at live events, you will have everything you need to help other women walk with God. I want to practice what I preach by truly coming alongside you in every way I can imagine to help you become a disciple who makes disciples who will make disciples. It's time to go deeper!

Deeper Waters

When I was growing up, I was told what to believe. My belief system was a set of someone else's beliefs imposed on me. I want to see the next generation discipled in such a way that we do not do their thinking, studying, and applying for them, but rather we teach them how to encounter God and listen for Him to tell them what to believe, and how to respond as a result. I believe the result will be confident young women with strong personal and biblical convictions that will stand the test of time and temptation.

Several years back, my family went canoeing for the first time, down a perceivably uneventful river. It appeared that it would be more of a lazy tubing experience than actual canoeing. We paired off in twos (my husband, Dale, and daughter, Jorja, in one canoe, and me and my son, Cole, in the other) and loaded up the canoes for a trip from one side of the river to the other, excited to see what lay ahead. I got in, steadied myself, and stuck my oar confidently in the water to "steer this puppy" down the river. I thought, *I am fairly coordinated, so this should be easy enough to maneuver.* Boy, was I wrong! I looked like a bug trying to fight going down the drain! Instead of forging ahead, I found myself going in circles, getting extremely frustrated, growing exhausted from the fight of the current, and watching as Dale and Jorja in the other canoe glided across the river with seemingly no problems at all. Cole tried to lighten my mood by threatening to splash me with his oar, and about the time I began to tell him that would not be a good idea, he doused me from head to toe. I was then tired, frustrated, *and wet*, feeling that I looked like a dog getting bathed: soaked, exposed, and just plain ugly.

I wanted to cry.

I finally got myself together and began to talk with Cole about how we could start this thing over and steer the boat better together. I humbled myself and let him lead in the cadences of *left, right, left, right*. Finally, we got into a rhythm that was taking us somewhere, and we were excited. We ended up passing Dale and Jorja, trash-talking to boot, feeling as though we were winning the latest concrete canoe competition. Our pride was quickly squashed, however, when we came around a corner and saw a turbulent drop ahead. We began to panic. I even remember saying that we needed to back off and let the other two go ahead of us so that they could show us what not to do. (Notice that I am throwing my own husband and child into this!)

Nonetheless, we were in front, and before we knew it, we were plunged into the frothing liquid instability. All I remember is simply yielding the canoe and the oar to the process and hanging on for dear life. We somehow made it through to the other side and got thrust into a strong current that literally carried us the rest of the trip down the river. There were still some experiences left to be had: We still had to work together, we still had obstacles to overcome, and we still faced threats to battle. Yet for the final half of our trip, I felt calm, relaxed, and peaceful. I even began to notice all of the beauty around me. I remember thinking, *This is how it was supposed to be all along!*

I wonder if you have experienced something similar in the spiritual as well as the natural world. I know I have.

I personally thought that being a Christian was completely up to me, and if I would just act right, which appeared to be fairly easy, all would be fine. Yet, as I grew, gradually learning there was more to this thing called Christianity, I tried desperately to get to the "other side," but I honestly just went in circles, becoming frustrated, tired, and envious of others who were seemingly headed in the direction I so desperately wanted to go. And about the time I started thinking that I was figuring it out, something hit me out of nowhere, threatening to destroy whatever headway I had made, just like getting splashed by Cole. The setback left me feeling disillusioned with it all, and either pressured me to quit or press on. I think this is where many of us get stuck—and we stay stuck for a long time: stuck in the lake of life, knowing that there's more, but not knowing how to get to the place of just yielding to His directives and enjoying the beauty of His presence along the way.

Jesus and the disciples found themselves in a similar situation, as penned in Matthew 14:22-33. Jesus had sent His disciples out in a boat on the lake while He dismissed a crowd of people and went alone to a mountainside to pray. The boat was getting tossed and beaten by the strong winds, and so Jesus walked out to them on the waters. All the disciples were afraid, but Jesus assured them that it was He and that everything would be fine. Then Peter said in verse 28, "Master, if it's really you, call me to come to you on the water." "Come ahead," He said.

Many a sermon has been spoken about how Peter took his eyes off Jesus and then began to sink. But what I see is one man out of twelve who had enough courage and trust in Jesus to step out of the boat. Jesus called Peter out, and he went. Of all the twelve disciples, which one do you think really experienced life in its fullest at that moment? Which one discovered a deeper faith in Jesus? And who went on as a result and established and grew the church, Jesus' bride, the dearest to His heart? You see, I believe it is not the one who tries and fails that is a failure, but the ones who never step out and try at all. Peter, as brief as it may have been, experienced walking on the water, joining Jesus in the deep. That's more than the others could say.

I believe that God is calling you to live deeper with Him. I believe that He has more for you in your relationship with Him than you currently are experiencing, and He wants you to discover it and take some others with you. And I believe that as you fulfill His calling and commission to go and make disciples, you will find yourself freed from the feelings of being stuck, instead stepping out of the boat into a great adventure with Jesus.

"Go and make disciples. . . ." God is calling you out. I am calling you out. Will you be among the cowards who stay in the boat, seeing the great need to disciple the next generation but resigning yourself to let someone else do it? Or will you be bold and courageous enough to step out of the boat and help disciple the next generation, giving you a new, life-giving purpose and offering life with Christ to another? The choice you make could help start a discipleship revolution across our nation that turns this world upside down for the glory of God.

Be a disciple. Make a disciple. Join the revolution! The pool is open. Jump into the deep with me. This is not some hypothesis or theory. I have lived it. It is real life. And it works! I promise that you will find a fulfillment, joy, and excitement in your walk with God that has been lacking for years. You will truly be living deeper, and loving every last minute of it.

I leave you with King David's words of praise and his charge to us from Psalm 145:1-13:

> I will exalt you, my God the King;
>> I will praise your name for ever and ever.
> Every day I will praise you
>> and extol your name for ever and ever.
>
> Great is the LORD and most worthy of praise;
>> his greatness no one can fathom.
> One generation commends your works to another;
>> they tell of your mighty acts.

They speak of the glorious splendor of your majesty —
and I will meditate on your wonderful works.
They tell of the power of your awesome works —
and I will proclaim your great deeds.
They celebrate your abundant goodness
and joyfully sing of your righteousness.

The LORD is gracious and compassionate,
slow to anger and rich in love.

The LORD is good to all;
he has compassion on all he has made.
All your works praise you, LORD;
your faithful people extol you.
They tell of the glory of your kingdom
and speak of your might,
so that all people may know of your mighty acts
and the glorious splendor of your kingdom.
Your kingdom is an everlasting kingdom,
and your dominion endures through all generations. (NIV)

May those who come behind us hear these praises from our lips and continue the legacy we set before them. In Jesus' name I pray, amen.

Deeper Reflections

1. Which of the seven truths (and "experiential guides") most speaks to you? Why is that? What will you do about it?
2. Do you have the faith in Jesus that it takes to "step out of the boat" and "walk on the water," joining Jesus in the deep? If not, what will it take to get you there?

3. This chapter asks, "Will you be among the cowards who stay in the boat, seeing the great need to disciple the next generation but resigning yourself to let someone else do it? Or will you be bold and courageous enough to step out of the boat and help disciple the next generation, giving you a new, life-giving purpose and offering life with Christ to another?" What is your answer? What will be your first step toward accomplishing this?

women from generations past

The Millennial generation is preceded by a number of other generations of the twentieth century. Let's take a quick look at these older generations that have played a great role in shaping the Millennials into who they are today.

. . . .

other names for the millennial generation

Generation Y

Generation WHY

Generation Next

Nexers

Millenniums

Digital Generation

Echo Boomers

Boomlets

iGeneration

Net Generation

Netizens

Gaming Generation

Next Hero Generation

. . . .

G.I. Generation (born 1904–1924)

Because they were a part of World War II, they defended their country with great self-sacrifice. This generation developed much self-respect. They believed in unity and thought it good and normal for everyone to agree, work the same, and look the same. Loyalty, hard work, patriotism, respect for authority, self-reliance, and a strong sense of civic obligation were characteristics of this generation. They put their trust in government, authority, and community. Their civic-mindedness caused them to be great winners and achievers. Leaders put public interest ahead of their own personal gain.

A high school education was sufficient to find a good-paying, secure job with good benefits in their early years. Because of this lower level of education than successor generations, their perspectives on life tended to be shaped differently from later generations. Friendly and optimistic, they reflected a strong community spirit. The family unit was always important, and children grew up as the center of their homes, offering a stable model for marriage and commitment. They are the most loyal financial givers in the church, tithing regularly. Thus when the church presented vision, their response was always, "How much will this cost?" They like things the way they are and don't like change.

Silent Generation (born 1925–1945)

Watching their parents, this generation grew to have a great concern for others and for their plight in life. Because of this, they have excellent relational skills, displaying sensitive, empathetic, and polite attitudes. They are nonjudgmental and open, and many worked in helping professions as doctors, teachers, and ministers.

Though this generation has a great concern for others, their philanthropic activity caused them to neglect their closest relationships at home and thus they have weaker family values and the highest divorce rate.

As for their participation in church, they are committed to tithing and desire Bible studies that are structured well, show preparation, and allow for discussion. They brought in the desire for the church to help with divorced families and broken homes to offer practical solutions for the complexities of life.

Boomer Generation (born 1946–1964)

They have commonly been called the baby boomers, and until the Millennials, this generation was the largest in America's history. Their sheer size caught the attention of businesses, schools, the media, churches, and other organizations for decades. Whatever this generation did, many would follow. They are the generation that brought us bell-bottom pants and minivans. They pressed the nation for housing and jobs. They lived more independently from their families and were willing to move in their quest for affluence, thus prompting many families to move to the United States, bringing various cultures and religions with them.

Most boomers were raised by stay-at-home mothers who were younger than mothers with children at home today. They are the Woodstock and the Vietnam generation that believed their way was *the* way. In the 1960s the boomers were countercultural and antiauthoritarian.

That self-centered, independent spirit became a self-centered, materialistic spirit in the 1980s, prompting boomers to lose their sense of need for God, His help, the church, and others. By the decade of the nineties, the importance of the boomers became apparent in the growth of New Age spirituality and the self-help movement, in their thirst for spiritual things. Evangelism in the church was then at its highest, and it encouraged this generation to look and live by the absolute truths found in the Bible. While many adopted these truths, they were very slow at applying them.

· ·

what's "out"	what's "in"
▪ Slow and unwieldy	▪ Streamlined and efficient
▪ "One size fits all"	▪ Customized for the individual
▪ Passive learning	▪ Interactivity and real time information
▪ Dishonesty	▪ Brutal honesty
▪ Playing "games"	▪ Authentic behavior
▪ Intolerance	▪ Open-mindedness
▪ Next week or next year	▪ Now

· ·

Gen X (born 1965–1979)

They were originally called the buster generation because of the dramatic decline in live births from the preceding generation.

Those in this generation are also sometimes stereotyped as pessimists, perhaps with reason. From an economic viewpoint, Gen X entered the job market during difficult times. It is hardly surprising that they are both cautious and pessimistic about their long-term financial prospects.

They value relationships with close friends and family, they deeply believe in marriage, and they desire step-by-step plans to help them succeed relationally. In misdefining love as sex, they have had a high level of sexual activity outside of marriage and thus the highest abortion rate known to date.

They tend to unrealistically expect to achieve what their parents and grandparents achieved much earlier in life without as much hard work for it. As for the church, because of their parents' absolute truth, they are more relative in their mind-sets. Fellowship and community draw them to Bible study, and they will more than likely go to a church where their children are best catered to. They learn better by stories of characters in the Bible and how they dealt with life versus an abstract theology that really doesn't help them in their day-to-day lives.[1]

appendix B

beliefs of the millennials

The Millennial generation is a group of young people whose birth years range from 1980 to 2000. This generation is actually larger than the boomer generation. Millennials are already having an impact on business, the workplace, churches, and other organizations. They certainly are having an impact on politics. The eighteen- to twenty-nine-year-old Millennials voted for Barack Obama in 2008 by a significant margin. Because of their impact in business, politics, and the church, they are simply too large and influential to ignore.

. . . .

defining life events
- Columbine High School massacre
- 9/11
- Enron scandal
- War in Iraq
- Nuclear threat from Iran and North Korea

defining life experiences
- Grew up basking in the "Decade of the Child"— children were placed on a pedestal versus the adage "Children should be seen and not heard."
- Fathers were more involved in their parenting.
- Came of age during a time of incredible societal change.
- Most "hovered over" U.S. generation. Have had unprecedented parental supervision and advocacy.

. . . .

We should begin by noting that not only are Millennials the largest generation, they are also one of the most diverse generational cohorts. That means that for every trend we identify in this generation, there are also lots of exceptions. But that doesn't mean we can't identify some key facets of the Millennials. Here are just a few characteristics.

First, they are on track to become America's most educated generation. Second, Millennials view marriage differently than previous generations. They are marrying later, if at all, and many cohabit at least once prior to marriage. Finally, Millennials are the least religious generation in American history. They may say that they are spiritual, but only a small fraction of them say that religion is important in their lives. The sad reality is that most Millennials don't think about religion at all. But perhaps the most amazing thing about this generation is their sense of hope. Consider their response to the simple statement: "I believe I can do something great." About 60 percent agreed strongly with this statement, and another 36 percent agreed somewhat. That was almost every respondent to the question asked, 96 percent in total.

Marriage and Family

How does the Millennial generation view marriage and family? One way to answer this question is to look at the characteristics of their parents.

Baby boomers wanted the best for themselves. They had a level of self-centeredness that eventually shifted toward meeting the needs of their children. They wanted everything to be perfect for Millennial children. There was a high level of parental involvement. Hence, the parents of Millennials are often called "helicopter parents." When Millennials were asked about parental involvement, 89 percent responded that they received guidance and advice from their parents. It turns out that boomers are helping Millennials make decisions about work and life. Sometimes parents sit in on job interviews and even try to negotiate salaries! While previous generations might have rejected such advice, 87 percent of Millennials view their parents as a positive source of influence.

This positive view Millennials have of parents extends to the older generation as a whole. While baby boomers tended to be anti-authoritarian, Millennials have a very positive attitude toward those who are older. In fact, 94 percent said they have great respect for older generations.

When it comes to marriage, Millennials are still optimistic about it even though they grew up in a world where divorce was common. When asked to respond to the statement, "It is likely that I will marry more than one time in my life," 86 percent disagreed. Apparently most Millennials plan to marry once or not at all. It is also worth noting that Millennials are marrying much later than any generation that preceded them.

Millennials also view marriage differently in part because of the political battles concerning same-sex marriage and the definition of marriage. When asked to respond to the statement, "I see nothing wrong with two people of the same gender getting married," six in ten agreed with the statement (40 percent strongly agreed, 20 percent agreed somewhat). Put simply, a significant majority of Millennials see nothing wrong with same-sex marriage.

The impact of technology on marriage and family is significant. The Millennial generation has grown up with the Internet, cell phones, and social media. It is easier than ever to call on a cell phone or send a text to other members of one's extended family. Posting pictures on Facebook allows family members to immediately see what is happening to children and grandchildren. Millennials are introducing their families to a variety of ways to stay connected.

New Technology and Social Media

The Millennial generation has been influenced by media and technology as no other generation. Social commentators made much of the influence of television on the boomers, but the proliferation of the

Internet, smartphones, and social media has had an even greater impact on Millennials.

When technology first comes on the scene, there are early adopters, then a significant majority, and finally laggards. Millennials fit into the category of early adopters. When asked if they agreed with the statement, "I am usually among the first people to acquire products featuring new technology," about half agreed and half disagreed. And even for those who disagreed, it is safe to say they did not fit into the category of laggards. Millennials are quick to embrace new technology.

There is one technology that Millennials always have in their hands: video games. Video game consoles are part of the industry that pulled in more than $20 billion in revenue in 2008. If there is one form of technology that is easily identifiable with Millennials, it is video games.

When asked how they most frequently communicate when not actually with the other person, they rated phone first (39 percent), then texting (37 percent), and then e-mail (16 percent). At the bottom was letter (1 percent). The survey also noticed a difference between older and younger Millennials. Put simply, the younger you are, the more likely you are to communicate by texting.

Social media is also a significant part of Millennials' lifestyle. Not surprisingly, the most popular social media site was Facebook (73 percent), followed by MySpace (49 percent) as a distant second. They also like to read blogs (30 percent) and write blogs (13 percent). But since blogs require more time and energy than other social media, they do not draw in numbers as large as Facebook and MySpace.

Although social media can be accessed in many ways, the most common is still by computer. Millennials use computers both for work and for personal use. Most Millennials (83 percent) use a computer for work and spend about seventeen hours on it each week. One out of five Millennials use their computer for work forty or more hours per week. And Millennials spend time on computers for personal use—from five to thirty hours per week. The average was seventeen hours per week.

If you put these numbers together, you find something shocking. The average Millennial spends seventeen hours per week on a computer for work, and spends the same amount of time on a computer for personal use. That totals thirty-four hours a week on a computer. Thus, roughly one-third of Millennials' waking lives are spent on a computer.

Religion and Belief System

The Millennial generation is the least religious generation in American history. They are more likely to have a syncretistic belief system. In other words, they will take portions of belief from various faiths and nonfaiths and blend them together into a unique spiritual system. This generation is less likely to care about religion or spiritual matters than previous generations. When they were asked in an open-ended question about what was important to them, spiritual matters were sixth on the list. Preceding them in importance were family, friends, education, career, and spouse/partner.

When asked to describe themselves, two-thirds (65 percent) used the term Christian. Interestingly, three in ten (28 percent) picked either atheism, agnosticism, or no preference. In other words, they have moved completely away from belief in God.

When asked if they were "born-again Christians," using a precise definition provided by the interviewers, only 20 percent affirmed this definition of belief and experience. And when presented with seven statements about orthodox Christian belief, the researchers found that only 6 percent of Millennials could affirm them and thus could be properly defined as evangelical.

A third (34 percent) of Millennials said that no one can know what will happen when they die. But more than one-fourth (26 percent) said they believe they will go to heaven when they die because they have accepted Christ as their Savior.

Church attendance has been decreasing with each generation, and most Millennials who attend church do so as seekers. In other words, they are at least spiritually interested enough to visit a church even though they may not be saved.

The Millennial generation presents a significant challenge for us as Christians. The largest and least religious generation in American history is here and making an impact. If the church and Christian organizations are to be vibrant and effective in the twenty-first century, pastors and Christian leaders need to know how to connect to Millennials.[1]

appendix C

a millennial in her own words

Welcome to the Millennial generation, the most educated and technologically advanced generation ever to exist on the earth. We are more ethnically and racially diverse than any generation before us. Most of us have created a profile on a social networking site. Sadly, only a few of us are religious, because we are not looking for rituals; we are looking for answers. Over half of us were raised by both parents, and with the deterioration of the family, we tend to stress parenthood and marriage above career and financial success. Our third most important priority is the well-being of others, because we have seen the devastating effects that greed can have on this world. We are the fourteenth generation since America achieved its independence from Great Britain, and we represent 26 percent of the population of the United States. We are larger than the boomer generation, and three times the size of Generation X. We belong to a generation that is heavily involved in teamwork; we will work together to avert every crisis that comes our way. As we grow, we will become strong leaders who are able to solve the problems we face. These daunting problems currently include overpopulation, skyrocketing unemployment rates, exhausted resources, a bankrupt country, and a dying planet. Yet I have great confidence in our ability to overcome all of these obstacles and anything else that comes our way.

The world population is now at 7 billion. The last billion were born in only the past twelve years. It is predicted that we will reach 8 billion people within the next eight years. We have the highest unemployment of any group since the Great Depression. However, I believe that with our educational background, we will be able to cut this number in half within the next ten years. Oil, water, and air are being depleted at a staggering rate, and the chemicals that are being released into our atmosphere are so outrageous that an incredible number of people are going to be diagnosed with cancer in our lifetime.

Our parents are just the opposite of who we are. In their teens and early twenties, they spawned the sexual revolution and brought promiscuity to the forefront. We have seen the hetero-revolution, the African American revolution, the women's rights movement, and now the homosexual revolution. Most of us have maintained a moral ethic that has not been seen in a long time. Crime, drugs, and alcohol use are down in our generation. While those before us have spent us into oblivion and have left us with the bill, we, on the other hand, have mostly sat patiently waiting for our time to govern. There are a select few of us who have been protesting the financial slaughter of our future caused by the greed of Wall Street; however, I seriously doubt that these demonstrations will have any effect on the "fat cats" of this world. With so many catastrophes awaiting us in our lifetime, where are we going to turn?

I am fully convinced that this world is ripe for revolution. I firmly believe that we are on the verge of a worldwide revival. Not seen on this earth since the mid-1800s, we as a generation have a unique personality that makes us creative, courageous, and open-minded. These personality traits provide a platform on which we are capable of change. Listening to and trying to understand new ideas in an old world gives us the opportunity to see old concepts in a new light. An open mind allows for new ideas and provides a strong sense of self. It gives us an understanding of whatever truth we might discover.

As a group, we have a rightly suited personality for a relationship with God. Our character traits as a whole are morally correct, and loving our parents and caring for others make us a natural fit for a relationship with Jesus Christ. I implore you, if you have never stud-ied the Word of God, to do so now. Open your mind to what the

Bible has to offer you. Try to put aside all the negative connotations that are circulated in the media. We are at the age now to discard as accurate or inaccurate any beliefs we have "inherited" from our parents. It's time for us to search out the truth for ourselves. The Bible is an amazing document that has stood the test of time and deserves your careful consideration.

Our generation has established Christian rock. For the past ten years we have filled auditoriums to listen to names such as Third Day, Mercy Me, and Casting Crowns. These bands have exploded on the music charts: Christian rock is the sixth most popular music genre in America today. Gospel music outpaces sales of Latin, jazz, classical, and New Age music. The music ministry is reaching thousands of people; however, the separation between the Christian rock genre and the standard church is huge. This gap leaves most of us high and dry, longing for a local outreach that we can call home. Those of us who have a Christian foundation generally go back to our home churches yearning for more complete spiritual understanding. Most of us are left holding the bag because we haven't any biblical foundation to stand on.

We are a disconnected generation looking for Christian leaders who can relate to our spiritual needs. There is no typical belief system among Millennials, and most of us who call ourselves Christian do so because our parents did. Most of us are theistic, and we struggle with basic Christian doctrine.

We believe that denominations and other religious labels are not important and that religion should address justice and equality. We are a new generation of Christians, and we have transformed into several smaller movements that are now influencing major congregations. We have a tremendous desire for therapeutic spirituality with a group of fellow believers who are like-minded. Just going to church and singing hymns is not enough. We want to go to church and commune with other people like a family. We want to have coffee together, listen to live music together, and not necessarily have the long, drawn-out preaching of a traditional church service. We want to learn about God in a small-group setting, and when we are all together we want to spend time in fellowship with one another. Most of all, we are in search of a deeper understanding of the Word of God in this disconnected, complicated world.[1]

—A Millennial Christian

notes

The Greek and Hebrew words referenced throughout the book are taken from *Strong's Exhaustive Concordance* (www.biblestudytools.com /concordances/strongs-exhaustive-concordance) and *The Blue Letter Bible* (www.blueletterbible.org/index.cfm).

Chapter 0: Deep Calls to Deep

1. Thom S. Rainer and Jess W. Rainer, *The Millennials: Connecting to America's Largest Generation* (Nashville: Broadman & Holman, 2011), 22.

Chapter 1: Agree to "Follow Me"

1. George Barna, *The State of the Church: 2005* (Ventura, CA: Barna Research Group, 2005), 51.

Appendix A: Women from Generations Past

1. Information in appendix A was gleaned from Thom S. Rainer and Jess W. Rainer, *The Millennials: Connecting to America's Largest Generation* (Nashville: Broadman & Holman, 2011).

Appendix B: Beliefs of the Millennials

1. Information in appendix B was gleaned from Dan Kimball, *They Like Jesus but Not the Church: Insights from Emerging Generations* (Grand Rapids, MI: Zondervan, 2007).

Appendix C: A Millennial in Her Own Words

1. Information in appendix C was gleaned from Dr. Kara E. Powell and Dr. Chap Clark, *Sticky Faith: Everyday Ideas to Build Lasting Faith in Your Kids* (Grand Rapids, MI: Zondervan, 2011).

about the author

JENA FOREHAND experienced firsthand God's power to transform a life when He healed her broken marriage in 1997. With a spirit of authenticity, Jena and her husband, Dale, began ministering to other couples through marriage conferences, retreats, and resources. She was next drawn to women's ministry and the incredible need for living in deeper relationship with God through discipleship.

Jena's passion for Christ is evident as she writes and speaks clearly, comically, and candidly to women. When not traveling with her husband and family, she focuses her time and energy on how to best partner with future generations in discipleship. Jena lives in Birmingham, Alabama, with her family.

Bible studies for the
LIVING DEEPER series.

Connect: Living in Relationships
Jena Forehand

Teach young women how to build strong, long-lasting relationships with others and God. This exciting experiential guide focuses on relationships and is filled with thought-provoking daily reflections and fun experiences especially for millennial women.

978-1-61291-465-7

Love: Living with God
Jena Forehand

Discover a love beyond your expectations. This guide includes powerful daily reflections, fun activities, and deep truth about the One who is love and living in His love.

978-1-61291-466-4

The Message Means Understanding

Bringing the Bible to all ages

The Message is written in contemporary language that is much like talking with a good friend. When paired with your favorite Bible study, *The Message* will deliver a reading experience that is reliable, energetic, and amazingly fresh.